SHRM
Q&A
SERIES

97

Frequently Asked Questions About Compensation

97

SHRM
Q&A
SERIES

Frequently Asked Questions About Compensation

with Answers from

SHRM's Knowledge Advisors

Edited by Margaret Fiester, SPHR-CA

Society for Human Resource Management
Alexandria, Virginia | www.shrm.org

Strategic Human Resource Management India
Mumbai, India | www.shrmindia.org

Society for Human Resource Management
Haidian District Beijing, China | www.shrm.org/cn

The Society for Human Resource Management (SHRM) is the world's largest association devoted to human resource management. Representing more than 250,000 members in over 140 countries, the Society serves the needs of HR professionals and advances the interests of the HR profession. Founded in 1948, SHRM has more than 575 affiliated chapters within the United States and subsidiary offices in China, India and United Arab Emirates. Visit SHRM Online at www.shrm.org.

Interior and Cover Design: Shirley E.M. Raybuck

Library of Congress Cataloging-in-Publication Data

Compensation / edited by Margaret Fiester.

pages cm. -- (SHRM Q&A series)

Includes bibliographical references and index.

ISBN 978-1-58644-356-6

1. Compensation management--United States. 2. Employee fringe benefits--United States. 3. Employee fringe benefits--Law and legislation--United States. I. Fiester, Margaret.

HF5549.5.C67C59 2014

658.3'2--dc23

2013037828

13-0640

Contents

Introduction 1

General References and Resources 3

Acknowledgments..5

Chapter 1. Bonuses 7

  Q: What is the difference between a discretionary
      and a nondiscretionary bonus? 7

  Q: Are length-of-service bonuses considered
      taxable income to employees?..7

  Q: Must an employer pay out a bonus to
      a terminating or already terminated employee?..........................8

Chapter 2. Commission-Based Pay 11

  Q: How does an employer calculate the rate of pay
      for employees who are paid 100 percent commission
      when they take paid time off?..11

  Q: How does an employer handle outstanding
      commission payments for a commissioned
      employee who is leaving the company? 12

  Q: What are "draws" under a sales compensation plan,
      and how do they work?.. 13

  Q: What are the components of a commission-only
      sales plan? 14

Chapter 3. Communication 19

Q: What is the best way to handle employees' requests for pay increases? 19

Q: What should be included in a total compensation statement?.....21

Q: Are employers legally required to communicate wage changes to employees? 22

Chapter 4. International Assignments.............................. 25

Q: How should employees on international assignments be compensated? 25

Q: How should taxes for expatriates be handled?......................... 27

Q: When an employee is on an international assignment, is there a requirement to withhold social security tax from his or her wages? 28

Q: Must expatriates pay income tax? 29

Chapter 5. Legal & Regulatory Issues:
Not Fair Labor Standards Act 33

Q: What should an employer expect in relation to a U.S. Department of Labor wage and hour audit? How can a company be proactive in the future?.. 33

Q: What happens to unpaid wages owed employees when a company files for bankruptcy? 35

Q: May an employer postpone employee's pay increases or bonuses for the amount of time an employee is out on Family and Medical Leave Act leave? 36

Q: Are companies required to reimburse employees' personal auto mileage for business-related trips? 38

Q. What are the rules under the Patient Protection and Affordable Care Act relative to lactation breaks? How does the Act affect employers in states having existing laws on lactation breaks? What if a company's collective bargaining agreement already provides for lactation breaks? 38

Q: What elements should be in an employer's policy on breast-feeding in the workplace? 39

Q: Why do employers offer severance packages, and what should they include?...40

Chapter 6. Legal & Regulatory Issues:
Fair Labor Standards Act...43

Q: What is meant by the term "exempt?" 43

Q: What is meant by the term "nonexempt?" 43

Q: What is meant by the term "salaried?" 43

Q: What is meant by the term "hourly?" 44

Q: What is the meaning of "salaried, nonexempt employee?" 44

Q: Can an employer change an exempt employee to hourly status to cure an attendance problem? 45

Q: What are the rules regarding compensatory time? 46

Q: How should an employer pay exempt employees who perform jury duty?..47

Q: If an exempt employee requests a move from full-time to part-time status, can the employer adjust the individual's salary down to compensate for the reduced hours?................47

Q: May employers classify part-time employees as exempt even if they do not meet the minimum salary specified in the FLSA regulations? 48

Q: If a company makes a long-term reduction in an exempt worker's workweek, will the corresponding reduction in salary violate the FLSA salary basis test? 48

Q: May an employer pay an employee on an hourly basis, even if the employee's duties qualify for an exemption?.........49

Q: What are the exceptions to the salary basis test under the FLSA?...51

Q: May an employer require an exempt employee to record hours and work a specified schedule?...51

Q: Is a company required to pay employees for their time spent going to mandatory drug testing? 52

Q: If a company has no work for employees due to a recent natural disaster, must the employees still be paid? 53

Q: Are companies required to pay employees for breaks and meal periods? Must companies provide additional breaks for smokers? 55

Q: Can an employer require employees to stay on premises during an unpaid lunch period? 56

Q: Must an employer pay an employee for time spent in a termination meeting? 58

Q: How should on-call, nonexempt employees be paid for the time they are not actually working when on call? 59

Q: May an employer occasionally reward exempt employees' extra efforts by providing them with additional pay? 61

Q: Are companies required to pay workers for time spent in new-hire orientation? 62

Q: If a specific certification is required in an employee's job, are employers required to pay for the time spent attending training to obtain the certification? Must employers pay for the course itself? 63

Q: When a nonexempt employee is sent to mandatory offsite training and meetings, what travel hours must be paid? 64

Q: Are employers required to pay employees for the time employees spend putting on their uniforms or protective gear before the start of their shift? 65

Q: What time should be included as "hours worked" when calculating weekly overtime? 67

Q: Can an employer pay nonexempt employees at a lower hourly rate for time spent on company travel? 69

Q: Is there a legal requirement to pay student interns? 70

Q: If an employer offers free housing and a weekly stipend, must the employer still meet minimum wage requirements? 72

Q: When the state minimum wage differs from the federal minimum wage, which must employers pay? 73

Q: May an exempt employee work a second, part-time nonexempt job?..74

Q: Are employees working a compressed workweek and paid biweekly entitled to overtime in the week they work over 40 hours?..75

Q: Is a company required to pay employees who work unauthorized overtime?..76

Q: Are companies required to pay overtime to employees classified as salaried, nonexempt? If so, how is overtime calculated?..77

Q: Must bonuses be included in overtime calculations?..............78

Q: Must employers count holiday leave, vacation, and sick hours taken during the workweek toward the overtime requirement?..80

Q: If a company has a nonexempt employee work two jobs with a different hourly rate of pay, how is overtime calculated?..80

Q: Can an employer require its employees to work overtime?......82

Q: Are supervisors allowed to change employee time sheets?...82

Q: A company participates in an annual trade show held on a weekend. Is it acceptable to allow employees to volunteer to work at the trade show booth?.............................84

Q: May an employer deduct a half day from an exempt employee's pay when he or she is out half a day due to personal reasons and has exhausted all paid time off?...........86

Q: May an employer make deductions from an exempt employee's pay for a holiday he or she is not yet eligible for?..87

Q: What are an employer's obligations relative to pay when the company must close early due to inclement weather?.....89

Q: What are the consequences of making an illegal deduction from an exempt employee's pay?..............................91

Q: May an employer require that exempt employees use their paid time off during a business closure of less than a week? If not, is it permissible to deduct from the exempt employees' pay for the time not worked?...................................92

Q: Under the FLSA, may an employer dock an employee's pay as a disciplinary penalty?..94

Q: When a company hires or terminates an exempt worker midweek, must that worker be paid for the entire week?........95

Q: What are the FLSA guidelines for employing young workers?....96

Chapter 7. Paid Leave Benefits (Paid Time Off and Sick Time) 99

Q: Must employees on military leave be paid? Can they be required to use paid time off or vacation time for their military service?..99

Q: Are employers required to pay out unused vacation pay to employees who leave the company? 100

Chapter 8. Payroll..103

Q: What is a company's obligation in terms of holiday pay for employees working compressed workweeks? 103

Q: How should an employer handle a final paycheck, taxes, and benefits for a recently deceased employee?...................103

Q: What issues should a company be concerned about before deciding to change its payroll frequency? 105

Q: Can an employer ask to see the Social Security card of new hires for payroll purposes?...106

Q: How should a company process pay for an employee who was hired, worked for three days, and then was terminated?..107

Q: How should a company handle uncashed paychecks by current or former employees?...108

Q: Should an employer pay accrued vacation leave at the rate of pay the employee actually earned the leave or at his or her current rate of pay?..109

Q: Can an employer hold a terminated employee's final paycheck until company equipment is returned, or deduct the cost from the final pay?.. 111

Q: Can a company hold a paycheck from employees because they did not turn in their timesheet? If not, how can the employee be disciplined? 112

Chapter 9. Planning & Design..**113**

Q: What are the advantages or disadvantages of a lead, match, or lag compensation strategy? 113

Q: What should be included in a compensation philosophy?........ 115

Q: What are some common types of differential/premium pay, and in what instances would an employer consider offering this type of pay to its employees? 117

Q: How does a company establish pay for an employee in an acting or interim role? 119

Q: What is the difference between job evaluation and performance evaluation? 120

Q: How does an HR professional create a salary increase matrix for calculating annual merit increases?....................... 121

Q: How should salary increases be prorated when an employee's review period is different from the normal time period used for such increases?...124

Q: Can an employer contact other organizations in its area to gauge merit projections or other compensation and benefits data?...125

Q: What are some sources for salary survey data for all industries and occupations?..126

Q: What are the benefits of and requirements for establishing a stock option incentive plan?..............................126

Q: What are total rewards strategies? How can an HR
professional develop total rewards strategies for his or
her company? 127

Chapter 10. Tax Compliance **131**
   Q: Are employers required to have employees complete a
new W-4 each year? 131
   Q: What is a 1099-MISC Form, who gets one,
and when is it due? 132
   Q: If we have employees working in more than one state,
what are our state tax withholding obligations? 133
   Q: What is the requirement to report wages of employees
who are collecting Social Security benefits? 134
   Q: Are bonuses taxable? 135
   Q: What tax issues should companies be aware of when
giving employees a gift card or other small gift? 135

Endnotes **137**

Index **155**

Additional SHRM-Published Books **165**

Introduction

This book contains frequently asked questions and answers gathered over the years by the Society for Human Resource Management's HR Knowledge Advisors in response to members' questions on various compensation related topics. The book provides short answers to questions about common compensation questions for the benefit of HR generalists or individuals new to the HR function, who may not be familiar with general compensation issues or legal and regulatory issues relative to the Fair Labor Standards Act.

General References and Resources

COBRA
See http://www.shrm.org/legalissues/federalresources/federalstatutes
regulationsandguidanc/pages/consolidatedomnibusbudgetreconcilia
tionact(cobra)of1986.aspx.

Fair Labor Standards Act (FLSA)
See http://www.shrm.org/legalissues/federalresources/federalstatutes
regulationsandguidanc/pages/fairlaborstandardsactof1938.aspx.

Family and Medical Leave Act (FMLA)
See http://www.shrm.org/legalissues/federalresources/federalstatutes
regulationsandguidanc/pages/familyandmedicalleaveactof1993.
aspx.

Patient Protection and Affordable Care Act (PPACA)
See http://www.shrm.org/legalissues/federalresources/federalstatutes
regulationsandguidanc/pages/patientprotecionandaffordablecare-
act.aspx.

U.S. Department of Labor (DOL or Labor Department)
See http://www.dol.gov.

U.S. Bankruptcy Court
See http://www.uscourts.gov/FederalCourts/Bankruptcy.aspx.

Acknowledgments

SHRM's Knowledge Center is a free service to SHRM members. SHRM's Knowledge Advisors are certified, highly experienced HR generalists who provide information resources and practical advice in response to SHRM members' HR-related questions. Knowledge Advisors develop HR-related content, including Q&As, for SHRM's website. We would also like to thank Jonathan A. Segal of Duane Morris LLP for his thoughtful clarification of the Q&As in Chapter 7.

This book is dedicated to the Knowledge Advisors.

Chapter 1
Bonuses

Q: What is the difference between a discretionary and a nondiscretionary bonus?

For a bonus to be considered discretionary, it should be at the sole discretion of the employer to award it, not an expectation by the employees. A discretionary bonus is a form of variable pay; the amount, requirements, timing, and announcement of the bonus should not be disclosed in advance, as this may appear to be a motivator or incentive implying that meeting certain levels would guarantee a bonus or reward. In a discretionary bonus, the employer determines after the fact that there is a reason for awarding a bonus, such as reaching company and financial goals, or chooses to reward an individual employee after exceptional performance.

A nondiscretionary bonus is the opposite of a discretionary one. The employer from the outset determines the standards required to receive a bonus based on meeting specific criteria. The employees expect to earn the bonus if they meet the standards. An employer's incentive pay plan that provides additional compensation for exceeding performance or productivity goals is an example of how nondiscretionary bonuses are executed in the workplace.

Q: Are length-of-service bonuses considered taxable income to employees?

As a general rule, bonuses and gifts are taxable, but this is not always true. Still, employers should be cautious. In terms of length-of-service awards specifically, cash given as a service award is taxable. In short, any gift to which an employer can assign a dollar value must be taxed. Gift cards, gift certificates, cash of all amounts (no matter how small), regardless of their purpose, are taxable income and must be included on the employee's W-2 at the end of the year.[1]

However, under certain conditions, awards do not have to be considered income. For service awards, the value of up to $400 can be excluded from income for awards given to employees for length of service. To exclude the value of as much as $400 as income, certain criteria must be met:

- The gift must be "tangible personal property," which excludes cash or cash equivalents, securities, vacations, lodging, meals, and tickets to theaters or sporting events.
- The award must be presented as part of a "meaningful presentation" (does not have to be elaborate, but emphasis must be put on the employee's achievement).
- The award must be presented under conditions that do not create "disguised compensation."
- Length-of-service awards must not be presented to employees for less than five years of service.
- The employee may not receive another length-of-service award (other than one of small value) during the same year or have received an award in any of the prior four years.

Q: Must an employer pay out a bonus to a terminating or already terminated employee?

Bonuses are not required by law, so whether they are required to be paid at termination depends on the unique circumstances involved and the terms of payout included in the bonus plan. When terms of payout are defined, the employee may forfeit a bonus under certain circumstances, such as requiring current, ongoing employment at the time of payout; current employment as of the end of the plan year; or terminations for cause. Generally forfeiture is an acceptable practice but should be made clear and documented in writing, as with all terms surrounding bonus eligibility.

Without clearly defined terms of payout, employers are wise to pay out bonuses to employees who have met the specific goals, objectives, performance criteria, and like criteria that were required for the bonus to be paid. Neglecting to pay bonuses when criteria set by an employer have been met is not a good practice and can harm employee loyalty and morale, as well as damage an employer's reputation in the community.

Chapter 2
Commission-Based Pay

Q: How does an employer calculate the rate of pay for employees who are paid 100 percent commission when they take paid time off?

A common issue employers struggle with is how to handle paid time off for employees whose salary is based on commission only. Although no federal requirement provides commission-only employees with paid leave benefits, employers that wish to extend this benefit will need to determine the best way to calculate the commissioned employee's rate of pay. Generally, commission-only employees are able to receive an advance, better known as a draw, on future sales that have not been earned or are not currently available. Once the commission sales are available and paid to the employee, the draw amount is deducted from the employee's compensation.

An employer can use various combinations of draws plus commissions to determine the calculation method for paid leave, but three options are most commonly used when determining how much a commission-only employee will be paid for vacation time:

- Use the minimum wage as the rate of pay for vacation or paid leave (also counts as a draw).
- Limit the total pay for vacation or paid leave to the amount of the salespersons' usual draw.
- Add the total wages earned (base, commissions, and bonus) over the previous quarter or other representative period, and divide by the number of weeks in the quarter.

For example, Sue has earned commission for January, February, and March and wants to take one week of paid vacation in April. One option would be to use March's earnings since it is the closest month to the leave and to pay Sue one week of pay that is equivalent to one week of her earnings in March. Another option is to average Sue's earnings over the previous quarter leading up to the leave. This would mean adding the wages earned for January, February, and March and dividing the total wages earned by the total number of weeks in those months.

Given that there is no federal requirement to provide paid leave, the employer can choose what the "representative period" will be when determining the rate for paid leave. However, it is important to select one method of calculation and apply that method consistently to all employees who earn commission. Ensure that your company's policy also clearly spells out how vacation is paid out to commission-only employees, either with or without a draw. Finally, employers should always check their state laws to determine if there is any state requirement to provide paid leave, and if there are any requirements pertaining to employees paid on commission.

Q: How does an employer handle outstanding commission payments for a commissioned employee who is leaving the company?

All wages earned by an employee must be paid upon termination, and by definition, commissions are considered wages. However, commission payments are unique and present special issues regarding the time that all final wages are paid. In most cases, commissions are delayed until payment for a sale has been received from the customer; therefore, it would be impossible to calculate the total amount due when payments have not yet been received.

Employers should pay any commissions due to terminated

employees upon receipt of payment from the customer. Employers will also want to review any employment agreement or commission plan agreement to ensure payment of commissions follows the agreed-on terms. A majority of states have laws that outline the specific requirements for the payment of commissions to terminated employees.[1]

Steps should also be taken to reassure the employee that all commission payments will be processed once all open orders are paid. The employee may receive several commission payments, because all commissions are due upon receipt and will need to be processed for payment to the employee. At the termination session, the employer may want to create a spreadsheet of all open orders, indicating the amount of the commission pay anticipated for each order. Reviewing the company's procedures for processing commission payments may also be helpful should an order fall through and a commission payment be lost. The employer should maintain open communications with the employee until all commission payments have been paid.

Q: What are "draws" under a sales compensation plan, and how do they work?

A sales draw is an advance against future anticipated incentive compensation (commission) earnings. This form of payment is a slightly different tactic from one in which an employee is given a base pay plus commission. Under a base-salary-plus-commission approach, although sales employees may still be required to meet specific sales goals, failing to meet a particular goal will not necessarily affect their pay because they receive their base salary plus a percentage of any products or services they actually sell. With a draw-versus-commission payment, typically the only way for the sales employee to earn a higher salary is to meet or exceed specific sales goals to earn a higher amount than the draw rate.

There are basically two types of draws: nonrecoverable and recoverable. In both instances, if sales produce an incentive amount in excess of the draw, then the sales representative receives the additional monies beyond the draw amount.

When a sales representative enters a new sales role, either in a new company or in the current company, a common practice is to pay a nonrecoverable draw (also known as a "guarantee") for a number of months. Guarantees are usually temporary in nature and last for no longer than a one-year period, enabling the sales person to build potential sales into his or her pipeline. This process is also known as the "ramp-up."

A guarantee is a compensation payment made in addition to base salary that is paid regardless of performance. Even if the actual incentive earnings remain under the draw amount, the monies are not owed to the company by the individual.

Alternatively, a recoverable draw is sometimes paid to each sales person to assist with cash flow between incentive payments. For example, employers often pay sales commissions earned in a quarter one month after the end of the quarter. To even out earnings, many employers pay a percentage of the monthly target variable as a recoverable draw each month. At the end of the quarter, if the sales representative's earnings are less than the draw amount, the individual owes the company the difference. The amount owed may be carried forward to subsequent quarters depending on the sales plan policy. Any amount still owed at the end of the plan year must usually be paid back to the company.

Q: What are the components of a commission-only sales plan?

The Fair Labor Standards Act (FLSA) contains an exemption from minimum wage and overtime pay requirements to employees employed in outside sales, as defined by the Code of Federal Regulations (C.F.R.), Section 541.[2] Outside sales employees sell employer's products or services to customers away from their employer's place(s) of business, either at the customer's place of business or home. Sales made from the employer's location (inside sales) do not qualify for the exemption. Similarly, sales by mail, telephone, or Internet do not qualify unless they are in connection with sales made by personal contact. Some employees performing inside sales and working in certain retail establishments may be exempt under FLSA Section 7(i).[3]

Sales employees have a direct and measurable impact on the company's bottom-line profit; thus, pay structures for sales employees are typically represented in the form of total target compensation rather than as a fixed salary.

Elements of a sales plan can be classified into fixed and incentive based. Total compensation may consist of either a commission-only or base salary-plus-commission component. Sales people may be compensated based on a mix of fixed earnings (base salary) and variable earnings (commissions). Businesses selling high-value services or products usually opt for a ratio of between 60 percent/40 percent and 80 percent/20 percent of fixed to variable.

In organizations where sales representatives have greater influence over the buying decisions of customers, a larger portion of the mix should be through commissions. Alternatively, base salary should comprise a larger percentage of the mix in organizations where sales representatives do not exert much control over customer buying decisions.

Factors to consider in offering a commission-only plan component include the following:

- The degree of influence the sales person exerts over the customer's buying decision.

- The mix of new business to account development.
- The business sales cycle.
- The behaviors to be encouraged (that is, a high-variable component may lead to aggressive selling, whereas a low-variable component may lead to complacency).
- The commission component may be paid based on a variety of performance measures directly related to the company's sales and marketing objectives. There are two types of commission formulas for determining percentages to be paid:
  - » **Flat.** The commission rate is a fixed percentage regardless of the amount of sales/revenue the employee achieves.
  - » **Variable.** The commission rate may fluctuate up or down depending on the employee's performance or the measurement used.

To calculate an individual commission rate for an employee so that 100 percent of quota attainment results in payment of 100 percent of the variable target, divide the variable target by the quota. Example: Variable target = $60,000, Quota = $3,000,000. Calculation: $60,000 ÷ $3,000,000 = 2 percent individual commission rate.

Though many employers pay commissions on a monthly or quarterly basis, state wage payment laws generally define protected "wages" and set forth procedures to be followed when compensating employees. Various state laws include commissions among the wages subject to the statutory requirements; however, the laws do little to answer questions regarding the following matters:

- How commissions are calculated.
- When they are earned.
- When they must be paid.
- What if any obligation exists to payout commissions upon termination.

To avoid potential disputes over commissions, it is advisable to work with legal counsel to design a written agreement clearly detailing the terms and conditions of the sales incentive pay plan. These agreements may be in the form of a clause in general employment agreements or as separate commission plan agreements signed by the employee.

Chapter 3
Communication

Q: What is the best way to handle employees' requests for pay increases?

Deciding whether to provide employees with a requested pay increase that lies outside the regularly scheduled compensation review period relies on several factors and does not contain a one-size-fits-all solution. Consider the following:

- **Does the organization have a policy relating to pay decisions and increases?** Employers that do not have a policy may want to consider how past requests for increases have been handled.

- **What is the organization's compensation philosophy?** Whether or not employers have written policies about pay increases, most organizations have developed an opinion or culture regarding compensation decisions. The philosophy may be as simple as "we do not grant any increases outside our normal merit increase schedule" or "we review each request on the basis of its own merit." The decision to grant the raise should be consistent with the organizational philosophy.

- **What is the job worth?** Think about the value of the job compared with other roles in the organization. Every job has a point at which the wage becomes unreasonable as it relates to the tasks and responsibilities of the job, commonly referred to as the job's salary range. For example, paying cashiers a wage equal to their supervisor would be unreasonable given the supervisor's increased job responsibilities.

- **How does the employee's pay compare with others in that role?** Is the employee being paid less than others who perform the same or similar job? Or is the employee in the same salary range as other employees who have similar tenure, performance, experience, education, and skills in the same job? All factors being equal, employees in the same or similar jobs should be paid the same amount; otherwise, legal concerns may arise.

- **What is the value of the employee?** This consideration holds special importance for employees who have been selected as high performers during a succession-planning process or for small organizations in which the loss of one high performer could have a huge impact on the organization. If an organization has already invested resources developing this employee, then considering the employee's request may be worthwhile. It is crucial for the organization to understand exactly what the employee wants and the consequences of not providing it. For example, often high performers seek greater responsibilities, job titles, or promotions in addition to the pay increase.

Human resources should discuss these factors with the manager to help the manager quantify the pros and cons in the situation. The final decision must be in line with the organizational policy, philosophy, and job worth and should represent the value of the employee to the company. Once this decision is reached, the solution should be proposed to all relevant decision makers and ultimately communicated to the employee both verbally and in writing. Communicating the reason why the raise is, or is not, being granted is recommended to help the employee understand why and how the decision has been reached.

Q: What should be included in a total compensation statement?

One way an employer can show employees the total value of their benefits and compensation package is to present a total compensation statement. Total compensation statements give employees information on the complete pay package awarded to them on an annual basis, including both direct and indirect compensation. Direct compensation can be defined as ll compensation (base salary and/or incentive pay) that is paid directly to an employee. Indirect compensation can be defined as compensation that is not paid directly to an employee and is calculated in addition to base salary and incentive pay (e.g., employer-paid portions of health/dental/vision insurance, retirement benefits, educational benefits, relocation expenses, employee paid time off). The more detail that an employer can provide, the more beneficial the statement. The following are common items to include in a total compensation statement:

- Salary/hourly rate.
- Medical benefits coverage—include amount paid by employee and employer.
- Flexible spending account information.
- Paid leave—include vacation/sick/paid time off (PTO), holiday, personal, bereavement, military pay, jury duty, etc.
- Disability insurance.
- Life insurance.
- Employee assistance program.
- Retirement benefits—include 401(k)/403(b), pension plans, etc.
- Educational assistance programs.
- Relocation expenses.

Q: Are employers legally required to communicate wage changes to employees?

The answer depends on state law. However, in all states employers that pay below minimum wage to tipped employees must communicate wage changes to employees. Employers in New York[1] and California[2] are now required to provide notices to employees communicating specific information regarding the employee's wage rates and frequency of pay. Other states may have implemented such a law since the publishing of this booklet. Employers should check with their state Department of Labor office for current laws regarding wage notices.

The Fair Labor Standards Act (FLSA) requires employers to inform tipped employees when the employer elects to use tips toward the employee's minimum wage requirement.[3]

Although these requirements do not currently apply to the all employers in the United States, it is clear that wage communication is increasingly becoming a hot topic for state and federal lawmakers. Employers that lack a formal wage communication practice should consider implementing one.

Communicating regularly to employees about their rate of pay can help resolve misperceptions or misunderstandings. Regular communication about pay rates can also help employees who earn variable pay, such as tips, commissions, shift differentials, and bonuses, understand exactly how their pay is calculated.

Below are some guidelines for creating an employee wage notice:

- **Frequency.** Wage notices should be provided to employees at the beginning of employment and whenever the employee's wages change. Ideally, notices should be provided on at least an annual basis.
- **Contents.** The notice should be short, not longer than a single page, and list the employee's job title, FLSA classi-

fication (exempt or nonexempt), base rate of pay, and any additional compensation the employee is entitled to, such as overtime, tips, commissions, shift differentials, or bonuses. Be sure to include the payroll cycle (for example, biweekly, monthly) and regular pay date. The notice should also include the frequency of pay, specifically if a different frequency exists depending on the type of compensation (for example, base wages earned biweekly, commission earned quarterly, bonuses earned annually). And lastly, if the notice is communicating a pay change, make sure to include the effective date for the pay change.

- **Q&A.** You may wish to provide answers to frequently asked questions. Many employers shy away from communicating wages because they do not want to invite questions on the matter. However, answering these questions not only helps engage employees, but also helps them understand how pay works at your company.

Providing clear, easily understood information to employees about their rate of pay gives employers a chance to build trust and engagement with workers and to clear up any misconceptions and rumors about compensation that, if unchecked, can run rampant in the workplace.

Chapter 4
International Assignments

Q: How should employees on international assignments be compensated?

The most common approaches taken by organizations are the balance sheet (or buildup system), negotiation, localization, lump sum, and cafeteria plans. Each plan is best suited to certain situations, and each plan has its advantages and disadvantages.

Balance Sheet

This approach is most common. The main emphasis of the balance sheet is to pay an expatriate comparably to incumbents in same or similar positions in the home country. Thus, the expatriate neither gains nor loses from a financial perspective.

A home-country salary (base salary plus incentives) is determined for the expatriate. Frequently, this salary is determined in the same manner as that for a domestic position, such as by a job evaluation or a competency-based plan, market surveys, merit, and incentives. This salary is then broken into four categories. The categories are taxes, housing, goods and services, and reserve (for example, savings and discretionary payments).

The employee is required to use his or her salary to pay the typical amount toward each of these four categories. The typical amount reflects consumption patterns in the home country as determined by surveys from various consulting firms. The employer retains any amount under the typical amount and pays for any amount over the typical amount for each of the categories. Organizations often provide a relocation incentive in addition to the salary because certain assignments and locations require more than comparable pay to motivate an employee to take the foreign assignment.

The balance sheet approach is most appropriate for experienced mid- to senior-level expatriates. Its advantages include keeping the expatriate whole from a compensation perspective with respect to incumbents in the same or similar positions in their home country. In addition, this approach allows for ease of movement between foreign assignments and back to the home country (repatriation). Conversely, the balance sheet approach is complex to administer and intrudes into the expatriate's finances.

Negotiation

The advantage of the negotiation approach is that it is conceptually simple; the employer and each individual expatriate simply find a mutually agreeable package. However, this approach tends to be relatively costly, and it creates comparability problems when an increasing number of expatriates are compensated with the method. Negotiation is most often used for special situations or in organizations with few expatriates.

Localization

This approach involves basing the expatriate's salary on the local (host country's) salaries. It is easy to see that the same position in different countries may have quite different salaries. This approach contrasts with the balance sheet approach. The localization approach also provides for cost-of-living allowances, which can be applied to taxes, housing, and dependents and which is similar to the balance sheet method.

Some advantages of the localization approach include ease of administration and equity with local nationals. Some disadvantages include the usual need for negotiated supplements and pay based on host country economics versus performance and job responsibilities.

Lump Sum
This approach uses the home country's system for determining base salary. In addition to the salary, the expatriate is offered a lump sum of money to apply to items that he or she values versus a specific amount for taxes, housing, and so forth. This approach is advantageous because it does not intrude into the expatriate's finances, and the employer does not pay for things the expatriate does not want. A disadvantage to the lump sum approach is the calculation of the lump sum. It may involve a complex and time-consuming analysis. This approach is most often used for one- to three-year assignments.

Cafeteria
Senior-level expatriates and those with high total incomes relative to base salary are often compensated by the cafeteria method. This approach can be more cost-effective than other methods. The cafeteria method is similar to the lump sum plan, but instead of being provided a single sum of money, the expatriate is offered a selection of options to choose from. Options might include a company car or employer-paid tuition for the expatriate's children. There is, however, a limit to choices and amounts.

Q: How should taxes for expatriates be handled?
Companies generally take one of four approaches to handling taxes for their expatriate workers:
- **Laissez-faire.** In this approach, the company is not actively

involved in managing U.S. and foreign taxes. Essentially, the employee is responsible for any taxes incurred. However, often the employer increases the expatriate's compensation to cover the additional tax expense.

- **Ad hoc.** In an ad hoc approach, the employer determines tax reimbursement on a case-by-case basis. Essentially, each expatriate employee negotiates his or her own deal with the company. This approach may work when a company's international workforce is small, but as the international program grows, the negotiation process can become cumbersome.

- **Tax protection.** In the tax protection approach, the company figures the expatriate's hypothetical U.S. income tax and compares it with actual taxes paid. At the end of a year, the company reimburses any disparity. If the expatriate pays less in taxes than he or she would have paid in the United States, the expatriate keeps the difference. A disadvantage of this program is that it can create inequities between expatriates in low-tax-cost countries and those in high-tax-cost countries.

- **Tax equalization.** In a tax equalization program, the expatriate's tax situation is neither better nor worse than it would have been in the United States. A hypothetical U.S. tax is withheld from each paycheck. Foreign taxes are either paid by the employer or are reimbursed. Although this program ensures equity among expatriates, it requires more administrative resources than the other methods.

Q: When an employee is on an international assignment, is there a requirement to withhold social security tax from his or her wages?

Social security is an international concept and a mandatory benefit in most countries, giving coverage to and thereby automatically taxing any worker earning income in that country. When an employee accepts an international assignment, double taxation may occur because most home countries require their citizens to pay social security tax on all income, regardless of where the income was earned. To alleviate this burden from the employee and from an employer that has a policy of tax-equalizing its expatriates, the United States has entered into agreements with 20 countries, referred to as "totalization agreements," which allow for an exemption of the social security tax in either the home or host country for defined periods of time.[1]

When a worker is ready to retire, most countries require that an employee have a minimum number of years paid into their systems to qualify to receive benefits. If a worker has spent a large portion of his or her working years in another country, he or she may not meet the minimum requirements of his or her country's system, or that of another country he or she paid into. Therefore, the agreements also "totalize" the employee's working years by combining all years worked in agreement countries and using that total to help meet any country's minimum requirements.

Q: Must expatriates pay income tax?

Employers should be aware that almost every country has some type of income tax that applies to all workers. In addition to the tax requirements of the host country, the employee is also responsible for U.S. tax on income regardless of where the income is earned. The Internal Revenue Service (IRS) has two provisions to help ease the tax burden for employees on international assignment.

The first provision is Internal Revenue Code (IRC) Section 901, which provides that if the U.S. tax is higher than the host country tax, the employee pays the U.S. tax.[2] If the host county tax is higher, the employee is able to take a credit, or the host country tax can be claimed as an itemized deduction.

The second provision is IRC Section 911. This section allows for the exclusion of a portion of the employee's foreign income from taxation.[3] The IRS sets the maximum amount of foreign earned income that an employee working abroad can exclude from gross income under this section, which adjusts annually.

If the employee is planning on claiming this exclusion, he or she will be required to meet either the bona fide residence test or the physical presence test. U.S. citizens may complete IRS form 673 to give to their employer to show they meet the qualifications.[4] IRS form 2555[5] or 2555-EZ[6] must be filed by the employee to claim the exclusion.

Generally, Social Security and Medicare taxes are deducted from wages of employees working outside the United States if one of the following applies:

- The employee is working for a U.S. employer.
- The employee performs the services on or in connection with a U.S. vessel or aircraft, and either the employee entered into the employment contract within the United States, or the vessel or aircraft touches at a U.S. port while the employee is working on it.
- The employee is working in one of the countries with which the United States has entered into a totalization agreement (also called a binational or bilateral Social Security agreement).[7]
- The employee is working for a foreign affiliate of a U.S. employer under a voluntary agreement entered into between the U.S. employer and the U.S. Treasury Department.

State income taxes can further complicate the situation. Each state has requirements on residency as it relates to income tax liability. The employee will need to contact the specific state to determine the tax requirements.

Employers should encourage employees to discuss tax issues with their financial advisors before beginning international assignments.

Chapter 5

Legal & Regulatory Issues: Not Fair Labor Standards Act

Q: What should an employer expect in relation to a U.S. Department of Labor wage and hour audit? How can a company be proactive in the future?

The U.S. Department of Labor (DOL) has the ability to audit employers at any time, but the most common reason for a department audit is a complaint from an employee. The DOL has also targeted employers in low-wage industries for wage and hour violations, particularly in agriculture, day care, restaurants, garment manufacturing, guard services, health care, hotels and motels, janitorial services, and temporary help. By understanding the audit process and following the guidance below, employers will be better prepared to survive an audit.

Labor officials typically provide little advance notice of an audit. However, an employer can request time to gather records. Usually, the amount of time granted will depend on the auditor.

A company representative should contact the auditor to obtain specific information about the audit. Key information to obtain includes the following:

- The focus of the investigation, such as overtime pay compliance, exempt versus nonexempt classification, or minimum wage compliance.
- The time period for records the auditor wants to view.
- The names of any employees who may be interviewed.

Gather the records requested by the auditor. Be prepared to provide documentation related to compensation policies and procedures. Keep track of what specific information was provided.

Do not provide records other than what the auditor requests.

Designate one or two company representatives to work with the auditor. Some employers choose to designate legal counsel. Other employers designate senior managers. These representatives will be responsible for providing requested documents, for arranging for additional records to be provided as needed, and for coordinating interviews.

During the audit, employers should be courteous to and cooperative with the auditor. It is a good practice to provide a quiet work area for the auditor.

At the end of the audit, the employer should ask the auditor to provide a summary of the results of the investigation. This information will help the employer review options for resolutions if any violations are found. If violations are found, employers are encouraged to consult with legal counsel before reaching a settlement with the DOL.

Employers can be proactive by conducting a self-audit, including the following steps:

- Reviewing job descriptions.
- Understanding the differences between federal and state laws, and ensuring that the laws are correctly applied to employees.
- Ensuring that Fair Labor Standards Act (FLSA) classifications are correct.
- Keeping accurate payroll records.
- Applying policies consistently.
- Making sure all records are complete and working to resolve any inconsistencies.
- Determining how to address any areas of concern identified in the self-audit.

In addition, the Society for Human Resource Management's "Conducting Human Resource Audits" toolkit has helpful information regarding the HR audit process.[1]

Q: What happens to unpaid wages owed employees when a company files for bankruptcy?

The impact an employer's bankruptcy will have on unpaid wages depends on the type of bankruptcy filed with the U.S. Bankruptcy Court. An employer's bankruptcy generally takes one of two forms: reorganization under Chapter 11 or liquidation under Chapter 7 of the U.S. Bankruptcy Code.

Under Chapter 11 reorganization, the employer basically asks the court to assist with a repayment schedule or with selling off company assets as a means of raising money to pay off creditors.[2] A reorganization under Chapter 11 usually means the organization will continue normal business operations under the protection of the court until the time it is able to resolve its financial affairs. The filing of a Chapter 11 reorganization should have no direct impact on payment of employee wages.

Under Chapter 7 liquidation, the organization is informing the court it is no longer able to meet its financial obligation to creditors and is dissolving the business.[3] With Chapter 7 liquidation, the bank will prioritize creditors into the order in which they are to be paid off. Under this classification of bankruptcy, when an organization owes wages, the employees then become creditors of the bankrupt company. As with other creditors, employees who are owed wages share in the remaining assets of the bankrupt employer.

With the exception of secured creditors, which are typically given the highest priority for repayment, creditors that are owed wages, salaries, or commissions are given a higher priority for repayment than other creditors. Each individual employee of a bankrupt employer is given a priority of $10,000 (adjusted to inflation every 36 months) of all wages, salaries, or commissions he or she earned up to 180 days prior to the organization's filing for bankruptcy. In some cases, assets will be sufficient to satisfy employee claims in full; in others, employees may be compensated for only a portion of their claims or receive nothing at all.

Because claims for unpaid due to insolvency do not fall under the FLSA unless the employer willfully failed to pay wages owed and filed for bankruptcy as an attempt to avoid paying wages, the DOL has no jurisdiction in this area and will not accept claims. Claims for unpaid wages resulting from bankruptcy are regulated by the U.S. Bankruptcy Code and fall under the jurisdiction of the U.S. Bankruptcy Court. Former employees owed wages by employers that filed Chapter 7 bankruptcy can protect their rights by contacting the clerk of the U.S. Bankruptcy Court in the county where the bankruptcy was filed. A "proof of claim" form will be used by the court to determine how much money will be paid to individual employee creditors. As creditors of the employer, employees may exercise their right to participate in bankruptcy proceedings.

Q: May an employer postpone employee's pay increases or bonuses for the amount of time an employee is out on Family and Medical Leave Act leave?

If an employer provides unconditional pay increases to all employees, such as cost-of-living increases, then an employee who has taken Family and Medical Leave Act (FMLA) leave is entitled to that increase just as other employees are. Employers that grant these increases on a particular date each year need to provide pay increases on the same date to those on family or medical leave.

However, "pay increases conditioned upon seniority, length of service, or work performed must be granted in accordance with the employer's policy or practice with respect to other employees on an equivalent leave status for a reason that does not qualify as FMLA leave."[4] Therefore, employers that grant pay increases after a certain number of months of active service may be able to delay an increase for a proportionate amount of time, as long as this approach is consistent with procedures for other types of leave. Employers must be sure their policies on pay increases and employee leaves of absence are fair and applied consistently to avoid claims by those taking FMLA leave that they are victims of retaliation.

The rules for bonuses are the same as those for pay increases: An employee's eligibility depends on how the bonus is structured and on what the employee must do to receive it. Per the regulations,

> if a bonus or other payment is based on the achievement of a specified goal such as hours worked, products sold or perfect attendance, and the employee has not met the goal due to FMLA leave, then the payment may be denied, unless otherwise paid to employees on an equivalent leave status for a reason that does not qualify as FMLA leave. For example, if an employee who used paid vacation leave for a non-FMLA purpose would receive the payment, then the employee who used paid vacation leave for an FMLA-protected purpose also must receive the payment.[5]

For example, if an employee bonus is based purely on production, and the employee is not there to produce, he or she may be excluded from eligibility, assuming those on similar non-FMLA leaves are also excluded.

As a result, employers must be clear regarding eligibility requirements for various types of bonuses to be certain they do not improperly disadvantage employees returning from family or medical leave.

Q: Are companies required to reimburse employees' personal auto mileage for business-related trips?

No federal law requires employers to pay employees' travel expenses when employees use their own vehicles for business travel. However, many employers choose to offer some type of mileage reimbursement for their employees who drive their personal cars for work.

The Internal Revenue Service (IRS) standard business mileage rate is generally used by employers when determining the amount to reimburse their employees.[6] The IRS mileage rate is a maximum rate that employers may use; however, employers may choose to use a lower rate based on business budgetary reasons. The IRS rate is adjusted annually for inflation and takes into consideration the insurance, maintenance, licensing, and fueling costs of the vehicles. Because the rate considers these issues, employees are not obligated to document separate vehicle use costs. If the employee records the dates, mileage, and reasons for the business travel, the IRS rate can be used to provide tax-exempt reimbursements. The IRS rate does not include the cost of tolls or parking; therefore, any reimbursement for these expenses should be handled separately from the mileage reimbursement.

State law may require employers to reimburse employees for business-related expenses, including mileage. Therefore, employers should carefully check their state law and if affected, have a system to reimburse all employees for business travel according to the state's law.[7]

Q. What are the rules under the Patient Protection and Affordable Care Act relative to lactation breaks? How does

the Act affect employers in states having existing laws on lactation breaks? What if a company's collective bargaining agreement already provides for lactation breaks?

When an employer is faced with both a state and federal law on the same topic, in this instance lactation breaks, the employer is bound to comply with both of those laws. Generally speaking, the easiest way to ensure compliance with both laws would be to follow the law that is most generous to the employee. Therefore, employers must be knowledgeable of both the federal and state laws on lactation breaks and ensure that the policy of the organization meets all the requirements imposed by state and federal government.

The same also holds true for collective bargaining agreements.[8] A collective bargaining agreement is a contract between the employer and unionized employees. In this instance, the employer would have an obligation to fulfill the promises of the agreement as well as to comply with the provisions outlined in federal law.

Q: What elements should be in an employer's policy on breast-feeding in the workplace?

This is a great opportunity for employers to demonstrate their commitment to families and to family-friendly work environment, and can be used as a recruiting and retention tool. A sample policy should contain the following:

- State the organization's support for breast-feeding.
- Describe how breast-feeding employees will be allowed time to express milk while at work. The frequency and duration of breaks required will vary, and work schedules may need to be adjusted to accommodate lactation breaks. Generally speaking, new mothers spend approximately 15 to 30 minutes every three to four hours to express breast milk. As a

result employers may need to allow more than the customary breaks and time frames that are allowed under their current policies for lactation breaks. Employers are not required to compensate employees for these break periods, and the FLSA is amended to reflect this change in policy.

- **Describe how a private area will be made available for breast-feeding employees to express milk.** The act defines a "private place" as a place, other than a bathroom, that may be used by an employee to express breast milk; the private place must be shielded from view and be free from intrusions from co-workers and the general public.
- **Describe additional services provided beyond the minimum requirements of the law, if available.** Employers can use this opportunity to create a room that demonstrates their commitment to a family-friendly work environment. Make the room as comfortable as possible, with a comfortable chair and tables. Many organizations provide sinks, refrigerators, parenting magazines and bulletin boards for baby pictures. Consider providing a breast pump to use in the workplace.
- **Finally, make sure supervisors are trained on the new requirements.** They should be supportive and encourage others not to intrude on the employees' privacy during this time.

For more information on your requirements to accommodate nursing mothers, see the DOL's Fact Sheet #73.[9]

Q: Why do employers offer severance packages, and what should they include?

Employers may choose to offer severance pay to employees who are terminated, either involuntarily or voluntarily. The primary reasons for offering a severance package are to soften the blow of an involuntary termination and to avoid future lawsuits by having the employee sign a release in exchange for the severance.

Common benefits in severance packages include the following:

- **Salary continuation.** Usually an amount based on years of service or position.
- **Insurance benefits.** Although an organization's insurance plan may not allow a terminated employee to remain on the group health plan, COBRA benefits may apply, and the employer may pay the COBRA premium (or a portion thereof) for a specified period of time.
- **Uncontested unemployment benefits.** An employer may agree not to challenge a departing employee's application for unemployment benefits.
- **Outplacement services.** Assistance with finding a new job or time-off flexibility to apply or interview for new jobs.
- **References.** An agreement on what information will be disclosed to future employers. Be sure to obtain legal advice before agreeing to omit information if there is a chance that the employer may, in the future, be held liable for that omission.
- **Miscellaneous.** Other factors that may be relevant to the individual employee's situation, such as loan forgiveness or transfer of an employer cellphone to the employee.

When offering severance in exchange for a waiver from the employee, employers should be aware that no enforceable waiver of statutory claims may exist under a few laws, such as the FLSA, in a private settlement between an employer and employee. In addition, the Older Workers Benefit Protection Act[10] has strict guidelines for waivers and only allows an employee to waive his or her Age Discrimination in Employment Act[11] rights if the waiver is "knowing and voluntary." Employers are encouraged to seek legal advice when drafting and requiring waivers for exiting employees.

In addition, some states have severance pay laws. Employers should be sure to check state laws for compliance.

Chapter 6

Legal & Regulatory Issues:
Fair Labor Standards Act

Q: What is meant by the term "exempt?"

An individual is exempt from the overtime provisions of the FLSA because he or she is classified as an executive, professional, administrative, or outside sales employee, and meets the specific criteria for exemption.

Certain computer employees may also be exempt. Except for certain highly paid computer professionals and outside sales employees, exempt employees must generally be paid at least $455 per week on a salary basis.

Q: What is meant by the term "nonexempt?"

Nonexempt individuals are not exempt from the overtime provisions of the FLSA and are therefore covered by the provisions of the FLSA. Such individuals are therefore entitled to receive overtime for all hours worked beyond 40 in a workweek (as well as any state overtime provisions). Nonexempt employees may be paid on a salaried or hourly basis.

Q: What is meant by the term "salaried?"

An individual who receives the same salary from week to week regardless of how many hours he or she works is "salaried." Exempt employees must be paid on a salary basis, as discussed above. Nonexempt employees may be voluntarily paid on a salary basis and typically would not have their pay docked if they worked less than the agreed-on hours, with the exception of time allocated to paid leave the company provides. Salaried, nonexempt employees must still receive overtime in accordance with federal and state laws.

Q: What is meant by the term "hourly?"

An individual who receives an hourly wage for work performed is "hourly." Such individuals, because of the method of payment, are classified as nonexempt and are subject to the overtime provisions of the FLSA. The only exception is for highly paid computer professionals who meet the specific criteria for that exemption.

Q: What is the meaning of "salaried, nonexempt employee?"

Employees are considered nonexempt and subject to the Fair Labor Standards Act (FLSA) *unless* they are shown to be *exempt* from the FLSA's overtime and minimum wage requirements by meeting three requirements:

1. Exempt duties
2. Paid on a salary basis
3. Paid a minimum weekly salary of $455 (subject to narrow exceptions).

Therefore, "salaried, nonexempt" simply means that overtime must be paid and the salary must amount to at least minimum wage.

An employee that "receive[s] his full salary for any week in which he performs any work without regard to the number of days or hours worked" is considered paid on a salary basis, according to U.S. Department of Labor (DOL) regulations, subject only to those deductions permitted by the DOL with regard to the salary basis requirement.[1]

An employee paid on a salary basis that does not meet the duties test remains subject to FLSA requirements, and is "salaried, nonexempt." In other words, subject only to a few narrow exceptions under federal law (which may not exist under state law), being salaried is necessary, but not sufficient, to be exempt from the FLSA.

Paying nonexempt staff on a salary basis is actually convenient—even efficient for some employers—particularly smaller employers that do not outsource the payroll function. For them, paying a salary is administratively simpler than tracking and recording all hours worked in a week, and adjusting payroll accordingly each pay period. Such employers usually open and close their operations at specific times, so the chance of incurring overtime is small.

Q: Can an employer change an exempt employee to hourly status to cure an attendance problem?

Paying exempt employees for the actual hours worked as a means to curb disruptive and undesirable attendance issues is tempting, but it can create a host of problems, including the loss of exempt status. Do not do it!

For a position to be classified as exempt from overtime, the employee must meet a job-duties test and a salary-basis test. The DOL Fact Sheet #17G states: "Being paid on a 'salary basis' means an employee regularly receives a predetermined amount of compensation each pay period on a weekly, or less frequent, basis. The predetermined amount cannot be reduced because of variations in the quality or quantity of the employee's work."[2]

Employers can impose unpaid suspensions for infractions of workplace conduct rules, but the DOL has made it clear that this provision refers to serious misconduct, not to performance or attendance issues. The suspension must be imposed pursuant to a written policy applicable to all employees. Employers will lose the exemption if they have an actual practice of making improper deductions from salary.

Employers do have options, however. When exempt employees feel they are entitled to come and go as they please, employers should be ready to enforce attendance standards without the unintended consequences of violating wage and hour employment laws. Determine if the job duties need to be performed at a set schedule or if allowing some flexibility may be an effective way to increase productivity and morale.

Also, review company policies and practices to determine if the organization has established policies for flexible scheduling, including telecommuting. If an employee has difficulty coming to work on time or needs to leave earlier than scheduled, allowing the employee the ability to "flex" the hours may resolve this issue. Telecommuting may help if the reason for tardiness is related to commuting issues.

Verify that the employee does not have a prearranged religious or Americans with Disabilities Act (ADA) accommodation that may explain why he or she is arriving late or leaving earlier than the regular schedule. If not, then let the employee know that if he or she chooses not to work the assigned schedule, you will charge the absence to the employee's leave bank for the difference between the time the employee was expected to report to work and the time he or she actually arrived. Then follow your company policy regarding disciplinary actions. Reinforce accountability, especially among those who feel that they are untouchable and can start and stop the workday at will simply because they are exempt employees.

Q: What are the rules regarding compensatory time?

The DOL describes compensatory time, or "comp time," as "paid time off the job that is earned and accrued by an employee instead of immediate cash payment for working overtime hours."[3] Although compensatory time off is an acceptable practice in the public sector, the DOL does not permit its use for nonexempt employees in private-sector employment: "The use of comp time instead of overtime is limited by Section 7(o) of the FLSA to a public agency that is a state, a political subdivision of a state, or an interstate governmental agency."[4] The DOL has published guidance to state and local government employees regarding compensatory time.[5]

Q: How should an employer pay exempt employees who perform jury duty?

Exempt employees must be paid a salary that is a guaranteed regular amount for each workweek, regardless of the quality or quantity of work that is performed or the number of hours worked as long as some work is performed during the week.

Under the FLSA, if an exempt employee reports for a full workweek of jury duty and does no work for his or her organization, the employer is not required to pay the exempt worker for the week. However, if the employee does any work for the organization, including checking and responding to work messages, the employee is considered to have worked during the workweek and is entitled to a full week of pay.

Under the FLSA, exempt employees who report for jury duty for one or two days during the week or for part of a day but work the rest of the week must be paid their full salary for the week.

In addition to the FLSA, employers should also consider the effect of state laws when determining how to pay exempt employees who miss work due to jury duty.[6]

Q: If an exempt employee requests a move from full-time to part-time status, can the employer adjust the individual's salary down to compensate for the reduced hours?

The salary can be reduced if the position still meets all the conditions for the particular exemption, including the minimum weekly salary of $455. This is a one-time reduction in weekly salary that is made at the conversion to part-time status. The part-time exempt employee must still receive the full weekly salary (now adjusted for part-time status) not subject to reductions because of the quantity or quality of the work. In other words, the part-time exempt employee's pay may not fluctuate from week to week. The FLSA allows reductions in employees' salaries as long as the reductions are not designed to circumvent the salary basis requirement. When an employee is paid less than $455 a week, his or her position does not meet the FLSA exemption requirements. In such a case, the employee could be paid on an hourly basis.

Q: May employers classify part-time employees as exempt even if they do not meet the minimum salary specified in the FLSA regulations?

Part-time jobs may be classified as exempt under the FLSA provided they meet all of the requirements in the law, including the minimum salary requirement.[7] The FLSA does not define part-time or full-time employment, nor does it specify the number of work hours a position must provide to be exempt from overtime pay obligations. As explained in DOL Opinion Letter FLSA2008-1NA, the law does not provide special or pro-rated minimum salary requirement for part-time positions.[8] Therefore, a position must still meet the minimum weekly salary requirements to be considered exempt, along with all other exemption criteria, regardless of the number of hours it provides.

Q: If a company makes a long-term reduction in an exempt worker's workweek, will the corresponding reduction in salary violate the FLSA salary basis test?

The DOL issued an opinion letter that addresses this scenario.[9]

The letter answers a query from an unidentified individual whose client wishes to reduce the workweek of certain exempt employees from 40 hours to 32 hours with a commensurate reduction in pay.

The salary basis test is one factor in determining whether a worker is exempt from overtime and minimum wage requirements. To meet the white-collar exemption requirements, an employee must meet both a duties test and the salary basis test.

Under the salary basis requirements, an employee must be paid a salary of no less than $455 per workweek. Being paid a salary means that the employee receives a predetermined amount of pay for each pay period, and this amount generally cannot be reduced based on the quality or quantity of work.

For more information on the salary basis test, see the DOL's Fact Sheet #17G.[10]

The opinion letter states that the salary basis test does not preclude a bona fide reduction in salary based on a reduction in the workweek as long as it does not reduce the salary below the amount required by regulations.

Unfortunately, the letter does not state how long the change in hours and pay must last to be considered bona fide. Therefore, if an employer is considering a change like this but is unsure whether it will last long enough, the employer should consult with an attorney and also seek guidance on related state law.

Q: May an employer pay an employee on an hourly basis, even if the employee's duties qualify for an exemption?

There is no requirement to ever make any position exempt. Employers need not automatically designate as exempt employees who clearly perform the primary duties of the job functions described under one of the exemptions. Employers who maintain strict control over requests for overtime work, for example, or who need to keep track of all employee hours for billing reasons, may find that payment on an hourly basis works best for them. In such cases, the workers will most likely be nonexempt by default, simply because they are paid on an hourly basis.

By definition, to be designated as an exempt executive, professional, or administrative worker under the FLSA, an employee must be paid on a salary basis. As a rule, paying an employee on an hourly basis makes that worker automatically ineligible for exempt status under the executive, professional, or administrative exemptions. However, the salary basis requirement does not apply to outside salespersons; teachers; practicing lawyers and doctors; medical interns and residents; computer professionals who are paid on an hourly basis at a rate not less than $27.63 per hour; and certain executive, administrative, or professional employees in the motion picture industry.

Another way to think of this is by remembering that employees are typically presumed nonexempt until proven to be exempt, meaning that all employees are covered by the FLSA's minimum wage and overtime requirements until an employer can prove they meet the special criteria for one of the exemptions.

The advantage of using the exemptions, of course, is the ability to avoid the cost of overtime pay for additional hours of work. However, if an employer cannot clearly show that a particular employee's duties and pay qualify for exempt status, the employer should classify that person as nonexempt.

Periodic self-audits of employees' exempt status are a best practice. Auditors often give particularly close scrutiny to the classification of low-level supervisory employees and high-level clerical employees.

Q: **What are the exceptions to the salary basis test under the FLSA?**

There are several positions with exceptions to the $455-per-week FLSA exempt-classification salary requirement. Here is a list of the positions that may be paid less than $455 per week:

- **Business owners.** Any employee who owns at least a bona fide 20-percent equity interest and who is actively engaged in its management.[11]
- **Teachers.** Any employee with a primary duty of teaching, tutoring, instructing, or lecturing in the activity of imparting knowledge and who is employed and engaged in this activity as a teacher in an educational establishment by which the employee is employed.[12]
- **Practice of law or medicine.** Any employee who is the holder of a valid license or certificate permitting the practice of law or medicine or any of their branches and is actually engaged in the practice and any employee who is the holder of the requisite academic degree for the general practice of medicine and is engaged in an internship or resident program pursuant to the practice of the profession.[13]
- **Outside sales.** Obtaining orders or contracts for services or for the use of facilities for which a consideration will be paid by the client or customer, and customarily and regularly engaged away from the employer's place or places of business in performing such primary duty.[14]
- **Motion picture producing industry.**[15]

Q: **May an employer require an exempt employee to record hours and work a specified schedule?**

In the DOL opinion letter FLSA2006-6, the DOL confirmed that an employer may require exempt employees to record hours worked without jeopardizing their exempt status.[16]

Some management staff and employees may be challenged by this fact; however, legitimate business reasons exist for holding employees accountable to such a requirement. For example, when there are billable hours or when an employer desires to simply track hours worked for performance and attendance purposes, it is the employer's business prerogative to do so.

The employer may define the work hours and hold the employee accountable to the specified schedule without affecting the exempt status under the FLSA. Often, employers establish core hours as a measure of flexible scheduling.

The best practice for employers is to have a written policy to notify employees of any established requirements. The written policy would state the requirement, in this instance, to record and track hours as well as the method for recording hours.

In addition, employers may implement a policy outlining work hours, the need to comply with recognized schedules and the ramifications of noncompliance.

Q: Is a company required to pay employees for their time spent going to mandatory drug testing?

The DOL does not oversee workplace drug testing, but the FLSA provides guidance as to what is considered compensable hours worked.

For various reasons (for example, per regulations, drug-free workplace, position relevance), some employers require employees to participate in mandatory drug testing prior to the beginning of employment or after hire. Employers are not required to compensate a person for any time spent on *pre-employment* drug testing. However, once the employee is hired, FLSA guidance seems to indicate that employers must compensate employees when they go for such testing. According to the DOL, "Whenever you impose special tests, requirements or conditions that your employee must meet, time he or she spends traveling to and from the tests, waiting for and undergoing these tests, or meeting the requirements is probably hours worked."[17] Because the employee must participate in the testing as a condition of employment, it will restrict the employee from performing other responsibilities. Therefore, the time of day an employee is scheduled for the testing (for example, before work, during work hours, or after work) does not determine whether the employee will be compensated. The facts that the testing is under the employer's control, related to the company business, and a condition of employment will meet the standard for that time being counted toward hours worked.

Employers should consider scheduling employee drug testing during normally scheduled work hours. This practice could avoid any potential overtime issues because of the additional compensable time spent participating in the drug testing.

Q: If a company has no work for employees due to a recent natural disaster, must the employees still be paid?
Whether employees must be paid depends on whether the employees are considered exempt or nonexempt under the FLSA.

Employees who are paid on an hourly basis are considered nonexempt from the minimum wage and overtime requirements under the FLSA. Because these employees are paid based on actual time worked, generally they are paid only when hours have been worked. Some states do have "report-in" or "call-in" pay laws that require employers to pay nonexempt employees if they show up to work and are subsequently turned away if no work is available. Employers should check state laws to see if their state(s) has such requirements.

To qualify as exempt from the FLSA's overtime requirements, employees must have certain job duties and must be paid on a salary basis. Salary basis is defined as the payment on a weekly or less frequent basis of a predetermined amount that constitutes all or part of compensation, without reductions for variations in the quality or quantity of the work performed.

According to Section 541.118 of the DOL's FLSA regulations,

> "An employee will not be considered to be 'on a salary basis' if deductions from his predetermined compensation are made for absences occasioned by the employer or by the operating requirements of the business. Accordingly, if the employee is ready, willing, and able to work, deductions may not be made for time when work is not available."[18]

Only limited salary deductions are permitted for time missed without jeopardizing employees' exempt status.

Exempt employees must be paid their full salary if they work any part of the workweek in which the company is closed because of a natural disaster. They need not be paid for any workweek in which they perform no work.

An employer has the option to require the exempt employee to take vacation days, accrued leave days, or other benefit days when there is no work because of a natural disaster. In other words, an employer can require salaried employees to consider those days off as vacation days. For employers to require exempt employees to take vacation time, there must actually be accrued vacation benefits available. If no accrued leave is available, the employer must still pay the employee his or her full weekly salary when the employee performs any work during the workweek. Many employers will allow exempt employees to "go negative" or advance leave time in these scenarios.

Employers should have a clearly written vacation and leave policy to communicate this requirement.

Q: Are companies required to pay employees for breaks and meal periods? Must companies provide additional breaks for smokers?

Federal law does not require employee rest breaks, but most employers would agree that a best practice is to provide short rest breaks as a matter of company policy. Because no federal law requires employers to provide such breaks, they are not obligated to provide additional breaks for smokers beyond the employer's general policy.

When employers do offer breaks of less than 20 minutes, the FLSA considers the breaks as compensable work hours that should be included in the total hours worked for the workweek and counted when determining if overtime was worked.

Similarly, federal law does not require meal breaks. Bona fide meal periods,[19] which typically last at least 30 minutes, are not considered work time and, therefore, do not need to be paid. When determining whether an employee should be paid for a meal period, employers must understand what is meant by "bona fide meal periods" under the FLSA. The regulations state the employee must be completely relieved from duty for the purposes of eating regular meals.[20] Ordinarily, 30 minutes or more is long enough for a bona fide meal period. A shorter period may be long enough under special conditions. The employee is not relieved if he or she is required to perform any duties, whether active or inactive, while eating. And an employee does not need to leave the premises if he or she is otherwise completely freed from duties during the meal period.

Having a company policy[21] is essential in explaining the details of meal and break periods to ensure there is no confusion about what constitutes a break or a meal period. The policy should clearly explain how many breaks are allowed for the standard workday as well as for the extended workday, the time of day meals and breaks are allowed and their duration, and the consequences of not following the policy. Policies can also come in handy if a situation arises when employees take extended breaks or meals. The DOL has stated that "unauthorized extensions of authorized work breaks need not be counted as hours worked when the employer has expressly and unambiguously communicated to the employee that the authorized break may only last for a specific length of time, that any extension of the break is contrary to the employer's rules, and any extension of the break will be punished."[22]

Employers should note that many states do require employee meal and rest periods and may have other provisions regarding pay for these periods.[23]

For additional information and guidance related to federal law, visit the FLSA Hours Worked Advisor website for meal and break periods.[24]

Q: Can an employer require employees to stay on premises during an unpaid lunch period?

There is no specific law that prohibits employers from requiring workers to stay on premises during their lunch time. In some situations, this type of requirement may be the best way to ensure that operations run smoothly. However, employers should carefully consider the wage and hour implications of having a policy that forbids employees to leave during lunch. Depending on the wording and application of such a policy, the time could possibly be considered "on-call" time and therefore compensable.

According to the DOL's FLSA Hours Worked Advisor,

> An employee who is required to remain on his or her employer's premises or so close thereto that he or

she cannot use the time effectively for his or her own purposes is working while on-call. Whether hours spent on-call is hours worked is a question of fact to be decided on a case-by-case basis. All on-call time is not hours worked. On-call situations vary. Some employees are required to remain on the employer's premises or at a location controlled by the employer. One example is a hospital employee who must stay at the hospital in an on-call room. While on-call, the employee is able to sleep, eat, watch television, read a book, etc. but is not allowed to leave the hospital. Other employees are able to leave their employer's premises, but are required to stay within so many minutes or so many miles of the facility and be accessible by telephone or by pager. An example of this type of employee is an apartment maintenance worker who has to carry a pager while on call and must remain within a specified number of miles of the apartment complex.[25]

The FLSA further clarifies:[26]

(a) Bona fide meal periods. Bona fide meal periods are not work time. Bona fide meal periods do not include coffee breaks or time for snacks. These are rest periods. The employee must be completely relieved from duty for the purposes of eating regular meals. Ordinarily 30 minutes or more is long enough for a bona fide meal period. A shorter period may be long enough under special conditions. The employee is not relieved if he is required to perform any duties, whether active or inactive, while eating. For example, an office employee who is required to eat at his desk or a factory worker who is required to be at his machine is working while eating.

(b) Where no permission to leave premises. It is not necessary that an employee be permitted to leave the premises if he is otherwise completely freed from duties during the meal period.

In summary, the key in determining whether the time is compensable is the degree of freedom the employee has from work duties during the meal period. Employers should be mindful of this key issue when developing a meal break policy. In addition, employers should always be aware of state laws governing meal and break periods, as some state laws may provide more protection for employees than the federal law does.[27]

Q: Must an employer pay an employee for time spent in a termination meeting?

The FLSA defines the time that employers are required to pay for their employee's work under the law. The act defines different rules for exempt and nonexempt employees in these situations.

Under the FLSA, nonexempt employees are employees who are paid on an hourly basis and are eligible to receive overtime when they have worked more than 40 hours in a workweek. The law has specific rules that discuss how an employer should pay for time spent in lectures, meetings, and training programs.[28] An employer is not obligated to pay for the time spent in a meeting if all four of the following criteria are met:

- The meeting takes place outside normal hours.
- The meeting is voluntary.

- The meeting is not job related.
- No work is performed during the meeting.

In this specific situation, a termination meeting is job related, it would be mandatory, and it is likely to take place during normal hours. Since all four of the criteria have not been met, the employer would have to pay the nonexempt employee for the time spent in the meeting.

For exempt employees, those employees who are paid a guaranteed weekly wage and are not eligible for overtime, the rules are different, but the time must still be paid.[29] Because exempt employees are paid a weekly salary regardless of the number of hours worked, there are strictly defined instances when an employer is permitted to deduct from the employee's salary. If the absence does not fit into the approved list of deductions, then the employer is not permitted to make the deduction. Specifically, the employer is not permitted to make partial day deductions from an exempt employee's pay. (The only exception to this rule is intermittent leave taken under the Family Medical Leave Act.) Therefore, an employer would have to pay a full day's wages for an exempt employee who attends a meeting. However, the law does allow employers to pay a partial week's salary in the terminal week of employment, and the regulations place more specific guidance on this rule, stating that the employer must prorate the salary into days, not hours.[30] This means, for example, if an employer decides to fire the employee on a Wednesday morning, then the employee should be paid wages for Monday, Tuesday, and Wednesday.

Q: How should on-call, nonexempt employees be paid for the time they are not actually working when on call?

Whether nonexempt employees must be paid for their on-call

time depends on whether they are "waiting to be engaged" or are "engaged to wait" as defined by the DOL Wage and Hour Division.[31]

Some employers require their employees to work on an on-call basis. The need for on-call scheduling is most often a response to the business needs of specific industries. According to DOL regulations at 29 C.F.R. Section 785.17, "An employee who is required to remain on call on the employer's premises or so close thereto that he cannot use the time effectively for his own purposes is working while 'on-call.'"[32]

If an employee who is on call is able to use his or her time freely and is not performing a specific assigned task, that employee is waiting to be engaged. The employee can be available by telephone if needed; however, because he or she is waiting (off duty), the employee is not compensated for that time.

An example of off-duty status is found at 29 C.F.R. Section 785.16 in the DOL regulations:

> "If the truck driver is sent from Washington, D.C., to New York City, leaving at 6:00 a.m. and arriving at 12:00 noon, and is completely and specifically relieved from all duty until 6:00 p.m. when he again goes on duty for the return trip the idle time is not working time. He is waiting to be engaged."[33]

On the other hand, when an on-call employee is required to stay at the workplace or is so near the workplace that he or she cannot use his or her time freely, the employee is engaged to wait (on duty). In such cases, the employee must be compensated for this time.

The DOL also offers examples of waiting or on-duty behaviors at 29 C.F.R. Section 785.15:

"A stenographer who reads a book while waiting for dictation, a messenger who works a crossword puzzle while awaiting assignments, a firefighter who plays checkers while waiting for alarms and a factory worker who talks to his fellow employees while waiting for machinery to be repaired are all working during their periods of inactivity."[34]

If an on-call employee must carry a paging device such as a beeper or cellphone, and the employee is relieved of his or her duties, the time is unpaid unless the employer has an on-call policy that specifically requires pay during such times. Federal court decisions have held that on-call employees are not overly constrained by a paging device. Therefore, the unpaid, waiting-to-be-engaged status could apply to those employees who are not required to wait near or at the worksite.

As with any nonexempt employee, federal law requires that on-call, nonexempt employees must still be compensated at or above the minimum wage and must be paid overtime for all hours worked in excess of 40 in any given workweek. Also, employers should make sure to check state laws on minimum wage and overtime.

Q: May an employer occasionally reward exempt employees' extra efforts by providing them with additional pay?
Exempt employees are not subject to the FLSA requirement to pay overtime at time and a half of the regular rate of pay. Employers are not obligated to pay overtime to an exempt employee, but may if they wish to do so—without jeopardizing the exempt status.

As long as the exempt employee is paid on a salary basis, an employer will have met the FLSA compensation obligation. Compensating beyond the salary does not dilute or nullify the salary basis.[35] Therefore, above the salary, employers may pay a bonus, straight time overtime (STOT), or even time and a half of a regular rate without violating the requirements for the salary basis test.

It is acceptable to track the time of exempt employees for the purposes of performance, discipline, and other organizational matters, but not for the purposes of pay. For that reason, employers that want to reward the extra efforts of their exempt employees often allow time off or special consideration at bonus time. Nevertheless, it is permissible to count the hours that an exempt employee works to compensate that employee over and above the salary basis.

Q: Are companies required to pay workers for time spent in new-hire orientation?

The FLSA requires employers to pay workers for hours they are "suffered" or "permitted to work." To determine whether an employer has suffered or permitted an employee to work, employers may review the DOL Fact Sheet "Hours Worked under the Fair Labor Standards Act (FLSA)."[36] According to the DOL, attendance at lectures, meetings, training programs, and similar activities need not be counted as working time only if four criteria are met:

- Attendance is outside normal hours.
- Attendance is voluntary.
- The event is not job related.
- No other work is concurrently performed.

As new-hire orientation is generally held during normal hours, is mandatory, and is related to an individual's employment, and some work may be performed (for example, completion of new-hire paperwork, benefits elections), you will need to pay the individual for time spent in an orientation meeting or training session.

If an employee does not return to work after new-hire orientation, the individual would almost certainly need to be paid for this time as hours worked. Employers should enter the individual in the payroll system with information provided either in the individual's new-hire paperwork or employment application.

If the individual did not complete tax forms or other necessary paperwork, you must withhold taxes as if the individual had claimed no exemptions and forward the paycheck to his or her last known address, which again can usually be found on the employment application or resume.

Q: If a specific certification is required in an employee's job, are employers required to pay for the time spent attending training to obtain the certification? Must employers pay for the course itself?

The FLSA's requirement for employers to pay for nonexempt employees' training time depends on the following criteria:

- The training must be voluntary.
- The training must take place outside normal work hours.
- The training should not be directly related to the performance of the employee's job.
- No work should be performed during the training.

All conditions must be satisfied for the training not to be considered compensable time.

Some of these requirements can cause confusion for employers. For example, if the training is outside normal work hours and has no job relevance, and no work is performed during the training, but the training is required for the job, is the training compensable? In most cases, the answer is yes.

However, if all things remain the same in the above example, except that the end result of the training—such as a degree or certificate—rather than the actual attendance is what is required for the employee's job, the training or course work is probably not compensable time. In other words, when obtaining a certificate is involuntary, but the course work or training that is one means to achieve the certificate is voluntary, the time spent in training may not be considered compensable time.

Whether the employer would be required to compensate the employee for the cost of the course work, training program, or seminar is a matter of the employer's policy, contracts, union agreements, and any relevant state law, as compensation is not currently required under federal labor law.

Employers should consult the DOL Fact Sheet regulations on compensable training time under the FLSA and may want to consult with their attorneys for further guidance.[37]

Q: When a nonexempt employee is sent to mandatory offsite training and meetings, what travel hours must be paid?

There are special considerations for travel time pay when nonexempt employees travel for training and meetings. Traveling from home to work in an ordinary situation is typically not compensable time.[38]

However, if offsite training requires nonexempt employees to travel overnight or away from their home community, at least some of the time spent traveling is considered time worked and is therefore paid.[39] When an employee drives, all travel time is considered work time. When an employee is a passenger in a car, plane, bus, boat, or train, only the travel time that cuts across his or her regular work schedule must be paid. Keep in mind, this time includes travel hours that correspond to the employee's normal work hours, even if travel falls on a day an employee does not normally work (such as during a weekend) or on a holiday when the company is closed.

For example, if the employee regularly works from 8:00 a.m. to 5:00 p.m. Monday through Friday, and on a Sunday the employee travels as a passenger on an airplane for a Monday meeting, the employer is required to pay for any travel time that occurs between 8:00 a.m. and 5:00 p.m. even though the employee is traveling on Sunday. There is no obligation under federal law to pay for travel time before 8:00 a.m. or after 5:00 p.m. Therefore, if an employee does not start his or her travel until 6:00 p.m., no compensation is required. But if he or she flies from 10:00 a.m. to 4:00 p.m., all that time is compensable. Some states have travel time laws that may have additional travel time pay requirements.[40]

In addition, according to the FLSA, when the employee is performing work while traveling,[41] such as completing prework for a training class or preparing for a meeting while a passenger on the plane, this time is considered work time even if it is outside the employee's normal work schedule.

Q: Are employers required to pay employees for the time employees spend putting on their uniforms or protective gear before the start of their shift?

Employers may have to compensate employees if these uniforms and gear are "unique protective gear"[42] and are "integral and indispensable"[43] to the performance of their essential job duties. Hard hats, ear plugs, safety glasses, boots, or hairnets are not unique protective gear.

The process of putting on and removing unique protective clothing is called "donning" (putting on) and "doffing" (removing). In a case that ultimately reached the U.S. Supreme Court, the appeals court ruled that the time spent donning and doffing unique protective gear was compensable, but that the time spent donning and doffing "non-unique gear"[44] was too minimal to be compensable. It also ruled that the time spent walking from the locker room to the production floor was compensable. On appeal to the Supreme Court, IBP Inc. challenged only the compensability of the walking time, so the appeals court ruling on donning and doffing still applies.

In its ruling of *IBP v. Alvarez*,[45] the Supreme Court decided that the time employees spent walking from the locker room area where they changed into unique protective gear to the production area was compensable, as well as the time waiting to doff. However, the time employees spent waiting to change into protective gear was not compensable.

In response to the Supreme Court's ruling, employers should do the following:

- Train front-line managers and staff about activities that are compensable and considered "hours worked" under the FLSA and Portal-to-Portal Act.[46] Verify that your training includes examples of all preparatory activities considered to be "on the clock" and preliminary to the principal activities of a given job.
- Review and update your timekeeping processes and policies to eliminate further confusion.
- Provide staff with examples of your organization's unique and protective gear standards in accordance with your industry or government safety regulations. In the *IBP v. Alvarez* case, IBP employees who worked in a poultry plant were required to don specialized clothing, including Kevlar gloves, metal mesh vests, aprons, leggings, and safety boots that were unique to the job.

The donning and doffing of specialized and unique protective gear are compensable. Walking to the production floor from the employer's changing area is also included as a compensable activity.

Q: What time should be included as "hours worked" when calculating weekly overtime?

The FLSA overtime rules require employers to pay nonexempt employees one and one-half times their regular rate of pay for each hour (or fraction thereof) worked in excess of 40 hours in a given workweek. "Hours worked" refers to actual hours worked during the workweek, excluding vacation, holiday, and sick leave. Below are a few examples of employee activities and how they are regarded under the hours worked definition.

Travel Time

An employee who travels away from home overnight is not working when he or she is a passenger on an airplane, train, boat, bus, or automobile outside the employee's regular work hours; however, any time the employee spends traveling as a passenger on a weekend will be counted as work time if the travel cuts across the hours that the employee would normally work during the week.

All travel compensable by contract, custom, or practice must be counted as work time, regardless of the previous limitations on counting travel as work time.

Training Time

Training time is not considered work time if all four of the following criteria are met:

- Attendance is outside regular work hours.
- Attendance is voluntary.
- No productive work is performed during the training.

- The training is not directed toward making the employee more proficient in the individual's present job.

On-Call Time

On-call time is not considered work time if the employee can use the time spent on call primarily for his or her own benefit. If, however, an employee is required to wait at the employer's premises or at a particular location other than at the employee's home, all the waiting time must be counted as work time.

Time not worked, whether or not it is paid time off, does not count toward the 40-hour threshold used to calculate overtime pay.

Travel Time

The principles that apply in determining whether time spent in travel is compensable time depends on the kind of travel involved.

- **Home-to-work travel.** An employee who travels from home before the regular workday and returns to his or her home at the end of the workday is engaged in ordinary home-to-work travel, which is not work time.
- **Home to work on a special one-day assignment in another city.** An employee who regularly works at a fixed location in one city is given a special one-day assignment in another city and returns home the same day. The time spent traveling to and returning from the other city is work time, except that the employer may deduct or not count that time the employee would normally spend commuting to the regular worksite.
- **Travel that is all in a day's work.** Time spent by an employee in travel as part of his or her principal activity, such as travel from job site to job site during the workday, is work time and must be counted as hours worked.
- **Travel away from home community.** Travel that keeps an

employee away from home overnight is travel away from home. Travel away from home is clearly work time when it cuts across the employee's workday. The time is not only hours worked on regular working days during normal working hours but also during corresponding hours on nonworking days. As an enforcement policy the DOL's Wage and Hour Division will not consider as work time that time spent in travel away from home outside regular working hours as a passenger on an airplane, train, boat, bus, or automobile.[47]

For more information about the FLSA, see the DOL's Wage and Hour Division's publication titled *Handy Reference Guide to the Fair Labor Standards Act.*[48]

Q: Can an employer pay nonexempt employees at a lower hourly rate for time spent on company travel?

The FLSA generally requires employers to pay nonexempt employees for time spent in work-related travel.[49] However, the regulations do not require that an employee be paid at his or her normal hourly rate for time spent in travel because this activity does not require the use of the skills and abilities of the job for which the employee was hired. Therefore, an employer may pay an employee for time spent in travel at a lower hourly rate than the employee's normal rate. However, employers should consider several issues prior to implementing such a policy.

First, if an employer chooses to pay an employee at a lower rate, this rate must still meet the minimum wage requirements under state and federal regulations. Multistate employers must ensure compliance with the different requirements in each state. Next, the employer must advise the employee prior to traveling that he or she will be paid at a lower rate for the time spent in travel. It is generally a best practice to include this information in a written agreement or policy.

One of the challenges to such a policy will be tracking the time to ensure that the reduced rate is being paid only for the time spent traveling. At a time when employees are regularly and consistently connected to the office through smartphones, laptops, and the cloud, many employees use the time spent at the airport or traveling to and from the hotel to take phone calls and respond to e-mails. These times would be considered work time and should be paid at the employee's normal rate. Therefore, tracking how each hour during "travel" is being spent could be difficult.

Another challenge to this type of policy would be the impact on those employees who are reluctant to travel. Employees reluctant to travel will likely be even more resistant to travel if they are paid at a lower wage rate during the travel time.

Finally, during any workweek that a nonexempt employee works over 40 hours, or works over eight hours in a day in some states, the employee would be entitled to overtime pay.[50] Paying a nonexempt employee at two different hourly rates during a workweek would require a recalculation of the regular rate[51] and the overtime rate for those nonexempt employees who are traveling, complicating the processing of payroll.

In the end, although employers may elect to pay nonexempt employees at a lower hourly rate (as long as it is not lower than minimum wage) for time spent in travel, it is important to complete a thorough cost-benefit analysis to determine whether the savings realized are worth the additional efforts, complications, and potential negative employee reactions that the policy may generate.

Q: Is there a legal requirement to pay student interns?

If the interns are "employees," they are subject to the FLSA and must be paid at least the minimum wage. Interns may be exempt from the requirements of the FLSA if they can be categorized as "trainees" as defined under the law.

In determining whether an intern is a trainee rather than an employee, the DOL has consistently applied the following six-criteria test, derived from a U.S. Supreme Court decision *Walling v. Portland Terminal Co.*:[52]

- The training, even though it includes actual operation of the facilities of the employer, is similar to that which would be given in a vocational school.
- The training is for the benefit of the trainee.
- The trainees do not displace regular employees, and they work under close observation.
- The employer that provides the training derives no immediate advantage from the activities of the trainees, and on occasion, the employer's operations may actually be impeded.
- The trainees are not necessarily entitled to a job at the completion of the training period.
- The employer and the trainee understand that the trainee is not entitled to wages for the time spent in training.

In addition, in a 1983 Opinion Letter, the DOL determined that student interns would not be considered employees if they receive college credit for "an internship which involves the students in real-life situations and provides the students with educational experiences unobtainable in a classroom setting." In a 1988 Opinion Letter, the DOL stated that students would not be considered employees when internship programs are "designed to provide students with professional experience in the furtherance of their education and training and are academically oriented for their benefit."

An academic credit requirement does not necessarily mean that a company is absolved of any requirement to pay the interns; the

DOL's six criteria still apply. Therefore, if interns fail to meet any of the above criteria, they should be paid as employees—at least minimum wage and overtime compensation when earned. Although earning class credit for the internship benefits the intern and can be required by the employer, class credit is not considered wages and should not be substituted for wages.

DOL opinion letters provide some guidance on when interns must be paid, but it is a good idea to consult with legal counsel when designing and implementing an internship program.[53]

Interns may also be treated as independent contractors rather than as employees, but only if they are, in fact, independent contractors. The Internal Revenue Service (IRS) provides guidance on determining whether a worker is an independent contractor or an employee.[54] The DOL provides further guidance on independent contractors,[55] volunteers,[56] and FLSA coverage.[57]

Q: If an employer offers free housing and a weekly stipend, must the employer still meet minimum wage requirements?

Although employers may offer free housing and a weekly stipend, they still need to meet minimum wage requirements. Under the FLSA 29 C.F.R. Section 531.29, board, lodging, and other facilities customarily furnished by the employer to his or her employees may be considered wages and credited toward minimum wage obligations under certain circumstances.[58]

Under 29 C.F.R. Section 531.27,

> "In determining whether he [the employer] has met the minimum wage and overtime requirements of the Act, the employer may credit himself with the reasonable cost to himself of board, lodging, or other facilities customarily furnished by him to his employ-

ees when the cost of such board, lodging, or other facilities is not excluded from wages paid to such employees under the term of a bona fide collective bargaining agreement applicable to the employees."[59]

In such circumstances, the reasonable cost or the fair value of the goods or of furnishing the facilities may be added to the employee's cash wages before determining the regular rate of pay.

"Other facilities" (29 C.F.R. Section 531.32) under this section must be something like board or lodging. They may include such items as meals furnished at employer restaurants or cafeterias or by hospitals, hotels, or restaurants to their employees; meals, dormitory rooms, and tuition furnished by a college to its student employees; and housing furnished for dwelling purposes.[60]

Items primarily for the benefit or convenience of the employer, such as business-related travel expenses and necessary tools or uniforms used in the employee's work, are not considered other facilities.

Employers should also understand that the definition of "board, lodging, and other facilities" does not include travel expenses when an employee travels to conduct business on behalf of the employer. When an employee is reimbursed for expenses incurred on behalf of the employer, such payments are not considered to be compensation for hours worked and are excluded from the regular rate.

Q: **When the state minimum wage differs from the federal minimum wage, which must employers pay?**

Employers must pay the higher of the two rates. You might think of it as having to comply with *both* laws: If an employer pays an hourly rate that equals the current minimum wage, but the state minimum wage is higher, then the employer would not be in compliance with state law. Likewise, if state minimum wage is lower than the current federal minimum wage, an employer would not be in compliance with federal law if it paid only the lower state wage.

Q: May an exempt employee work a second, part-time nonexempt job?

Although employees may perform more than one job for an employer, an employee may only have one FLSA designation—either exempt or nonexempt. If an employee wishes to work two different jobs for an employer, the exemption status must be based on the combination of the two jobs' duties as if the employee were performing one job. The "primary duty" as described under 29 C.F.R. Section 547.700 must be that of exempt work for a position to be considered exempt.[61] When looking at all the duties of the combined positions, if the "job" still meets the exemption criteria under the FLSA, then the employee may retain his or her exempt status; if not, the employee would lose the exemption status for both jobs and would have to be reclassified as nonexempt for both jobs.

If the combined duties would still qualify the employee to remain in an exempt status, the FLSA would not require the employer to pay the employee any additional salary above the normal weekly salary, and it would not prohibit an employer from paying more for the additional work, in any increment or method chosen (for example, hourly, day rate, piece rate). The only requirement would be to pay the employee his or her current, regular salary, which meets the salary basis test under the FLSA. Clearly, not many employees would voluntarily take on a second job without additional compensation, so employers that customarily allow such an arrangement would pay an additional hourly rate for the hours worked at the second job, but they would not be required to pay any overtime.

If the combined duties of the two jobs would no longer allow the employee to remain in an exempt status, the employee would become nonexempt for both jobs, and overtime would need to be paid on all hours worked over 40 in a week. (Some state laws may have daily overtime requirements.) The basic rate on which to compute the overtime would be either the weighted average of the two wages or the rate of the job in which the overtime was earned. (Some states may have more stringent laws for calculating basic rates for two or more jobs.) This approach could become quite expensive for an employer and would certainly pose an additional administrative burden.

Employers are not required to allow employees to work more than one job for them; employers may choose to allow or prohibit this arrangement and may set their own criteria for doing so, as long as they do not discriminate against a protected class. Either way, a well-written policy would be advisable to clearly communicate the employer's policy on the issue and to ward off any unintended discrimination.

Q: Are employees working a compressed workweek and paid biweekly entitled to overtime in the week they work over 40 hours?

Generally speaking, yes, although there are a few exceptions. Per the FLSA, all hours worked over 40 in an established workweek must be paid at one and one-half times the regular rate of pay. Additionally, some states have daily overtime payment requirements of up to double the regular rate. Taking those requirements into consideration, most compressed workweeks would incur overtime during one of the two weeks of the pay period. One exception is found within the medical profession, which has a statutory exception for hospitals for people who are sick, elderly, or have mental illness, often referred to as an 8/80 plan, to allow overtime to be paid either daily, for any hours worked over eight in a day, or biweekly, for any hours worked over 80 in a 14-day period, whichever is greater.[62] State daily overtime pay requirements still apply, however, and need to be considered in the overtime calculations.

The other possible solution, given the situation, would be to permanently adjust the defined workweek. For example, if employees are working four nine-hour days Monday through Thursday, and one eight-hour day every other Friday, their workweek would be 44-hours the first week and 36-hours the second. The FLSA requires employers to pay overtime for any hours worked over 40 in a workweek, but it only defines "workweek" as a fixed and recurring period of 168 hours composed of seven consecutive 24-hour periods.[63] If the workweek for the above schedule were established as Friday at noon to the following Friday at noon, then only 40 hours would actually be worked each workweek, and no overtime would be incurred for federal purposes. Of course, state daily overtime requirements would still apply and would need to be complied with.

Q: Is a company required to pay employees who work unauthorized overtime?

According to 29 C.F.R. Section 785.11 of the FLSA regulations,

> "Work not requested but suffered or permitted is work time. For example, an employee may voluntarily continue to work at the end of the shift. He may be a pieceworker, he may desire to finish an assigned task or he may wish to correct errors, paste work tickets, and prepare time reports or other records. The reason is immaterial. The employer knows or has reason to believe that he is continuing to work and the time is working time."[64]

Furthermore, 29 C.F.R. Section 785.13 of the regulations states,
"In all such cases it is the duty of the manage-
ment to exercise its control and see that the work
is not performed if it does not want it to be performed. It cannot sit back and accept the benefits
without compensating for them. The mere promul-
gation of a rule against such work is not enough.
Management has the power to enforce the rule and
must make every effort to do so."[65]

As the above regulatory language indicates, even a clearly communicated policy prohibiting unauthorized overtime does not relieve
an employer from its legal obligation to pay employees for all hours
worked. Therefore, if the employer allows the employee to perform
the work, the employer is liable for compensating the employee.

However, the FLSA does not prohibit employers from implementing a policy or enforcing an existing policy that prohibits
unauthorized work, and it does not prohibit employers from disci-
plining employees for violating the policy.

Employers wishing to avoid the legal liability of paying for
unauthorized overtime can actively discourage employees from
working extra hours by designing, implementing, and enforcing
a clearly communicated policy as well as by providing managers
and supervisors with appropriate training to better prepare them
to enforce the policy in a consistent manner.

Q: Are companies required to pay overtime to employees classified as salaried, nonexempt? If so, how is overtime calculated?

Yes. Salaried, nonexempt employees are not exempt from the FLSA
overtime requirements. Under the FLSA, employees are either exempt

or nonexempt from the minimum wage and overtime requirements of the Act. To be considered exempt, an employee must meet both a salary basis test[66] (generally a guaranteed salary of $455 per week) and a duties test.[67]

An employee may be classified as nonexempt and be paid on a salary basis, but the employee will remain subject to FLSA overtime requirements. Such employees are commonly referred to as "salaried, nonexempt." Employers often err in assuming that overtime is not required for such employees. Salaried, nonexempt employees must still receive overtime in accordance with federal and state laws.

To calculate overtime for a salaried, nonexempt employee, first determine the employee's hourly rate. For example, an individual who earns a salary of $36,000.00 per year earns the equivalent of $17.30 per hour, based on a 40-hour workweek. The overtime rate for salaried, nonexempt employees is the same as for hourly nonexempt employees: one and one half times the hourly rate. Therefore, the individual with a 40-hour workweek would earn $25.95 for every hour worked over 40 in a workweek.

Employers should check their state overtime laws; some states have overtime requirements that are stricter than federal requirements. The stricter law must be obeyed.[68]

Q: Must bonuses be included in overtime calculations?

Nondiscretionary bonuses must be included, but discretionary bonuses may generally be excluded.

Nondiscretionary bonuses[69] are bonuses that the employer is obligated to pay, and they must be included in overtime pay calculations. Examples of nondiscretionary bonuses include bonuses promised in an agreement (such as an employment contract or collective bargaining agreement), bonuses tied to performance evaluations, incentive plan bonuses, or any bonuses based on a set criteria for an employee, a group, or an entire company.

Nondiscretionary bonuses also include service anniversary bonuses, attendance bonuses, bonuses tied to working undesirable shifts (sometimes in the form of shift differentials), production-oriented bonuses, and retention bonuses.

Discretionary bonuses[70] are not considered overtime-eligible, as defined in FLSA 29 C.F.R. Section 778.208-215.[71] To be considered a discretionary bonus, all four criteria must apply:

- The employer retains discretion about whether the bonus will be paid.
- The employer retains discretion on the amount of the bonus.
- The employer retains discretion about whether a bonus will be provided near the time frame it covers.
- The bonus must not be paid pursuant to any prior contract, agreement, or promise.

Examples of discretionary bonuses employers may be able to exclude from overtime pay are holiday or gift bonuses, spontaneous bonuses (sometimes referred to as "spot" awards), and percentage-of-total-earnings bonuses (bonuses based on total compensation earned during a specific time frame).

Employer actions can cause these types of bonuses to lose discretionary status. For example, an employer that announces in the first quarter that it will pay a holiday bonus in the third quarter may have transformed an otherwise discretionary bonus into a nondiscretionary one because there is now a promise to provide a bonus.

Employers may generally exclude contributions made to bona fide profit-sharing plans, trusts, or bona fide thrift or savings plans from overtime pay calculations.

The calculation of bonuses required to be included in overtime pay is explained in 29 C.F.R. Section 778.209.[72]

Q: Must employers count holiday leave, vacation, and sick hours taken during the workweek toward the overtime requirement?

The FLSA requires employers to pay nonexempt employees time and one half of the employees' regular rate of pay for all hours worked over 40 in a workweek. Employers do not have to count paid holidays, paid time off (PTO), vacation, personal, and sick leave hours taken by an employee toward the calculation of the overtime requirement, because these hours are not actually "worked" and are therefore not considered as hours counted toward overtime under the FLSA.[73]

Q: If a company has a nonexempt employee work two jobs with a different hourly rate of pay, how is overtime calculated?

Under federal law, an employer may take one of two approaches when handling this situation. The first method involves paying overtime based on the "regular rate," also referred to as the "weighted average."

To determine the regular rate, the total amount earned by the employee in both straight-time pay rates is divided by the total number of hours worked in that specific workweek.

For example, the employee works a 38-hour week in his or her primary job and is paid $12.00 per hour. In that same week, the employee works 12 hours in his or her secondary position and is paid $9.00 per hour. The total number of hours worked is 50; therefore, the employee has worked 10 hours of overtime.

With any nonexempt employee, federal law requires that overtime74 be paid for all hours worked in excess of 40 in any given workweek. To determine the regular rate, the calculation is as follows:

38 hours x $12.00 = $456.00
12 hours x $9.00 = $108.00
$456.00 + $108.00 = $564.00
$564.00/50 hours worked = $11.28 per hour
$11.28 is the regular rate.

To determine this employee's overtime half-rate, follow these steps:

$11.28 x 0.5 = $5.64
$5.64 x 10 overtime hours = $56.40

This employee's total wages for the week will be $564.00 plus $56.40, which equals $620.40.

When calculating overtime using the second method, the employer and employee must reach an agreement in advance of the hours worked. They may agree to pay the employee one and one-half times the hourly nonovertime rate for all overtime hours worked based on the position worked when the overtime hours occurred.

Using the previous example, if the employee worked in the position that paid $9.00 per hour during all overtime hours, the overtime is paid using the $9.00-per-hour straight rate and an overtime rate of $13.50 ($9.00 x 0.5 = $4.50; $9.00 + $4.50 = $13.50). The employee then earns $456.00 for the time worked in his or her primary position, $18.00 for the two straight hours worked in the secondary position (2 hours x $9.00), and $135.00 for the ten hours of overtime (10 hours x $13.50) for a grand total of $609.00.

Q: Can an employer require its employees to work over-time?

Absent a collective bargaining agreement to the contrary, it is generally accepted that management has the right to require employees to work overtime when business conditions make such scheduling necessary. In exercising this right, employers must be reasonable and fair, ensuring that mandatory overtime is used only for legitimate business needs. Employees should be advised and regularly reminded of the company's policy on mandatory overtime. Employers should ensure that employers understand the conditions for its use and the consequences of not complying with the policy. Refusal to work overtime should be treated as any other rule violation, and appropriate discipline should be applied. In turn, employers should make every attempt to provide reasonable notice of the need for overtime.

Employers should be sensitive to the needs of employees and consider legitimate excuses fairly and consistently. Seek volunteers for overtime before initiating mandatory overtime. Employers should familiarize themselves with the laws regarding overtime and meal and rest periods in the states in which they operate. It is recommended that employers consult with an attorney in developing and implementing a policy on mandatory overtime, as they should with any new policy.

Q: Are supervisors allowed to change employee time sheets?

Under the FLSA, covered employers must keep certain records for nonexempt employees, including hours worked each day and total hours worked each workweek. To do so, employers may use any timekeeping method, including timesheets, time clocks, or automated timekeeping systems. Employers may allow supervisors to keep track of their employees' work hours, have employees track their own time, or both. Under the FLSA, however, employers—not the employees—have the ultimate responsibility to maintain these records. For this reason, employers have the ability to change employee time records but must ensure that the records accurately reflect the time actually worked.

There are only certain times when employers should change employee time records. For example, an employee may forget to record his or her start time on a timesheet or forget to punch in on a time clock. In this case, an employer may enter the employee's time on either record to ensure the employee is paid correctly. Another example is when an employee is out sick. The employer may change the time record to reflect a paid sick day instead of time worked. However, an employer may not change a time record to show fewer hours than actually worked. For example, an employer may not change an employee's time record from 48 hours to 40 hours in a workweek to avoid overtime payment, even if an employee were to consent to the change. In addition, an employer may not change an employee's time record to remove hours worked. For example, if an employee voluntarily continues to work after the end of his or her shift to complete an assignment, this work—even though not requested but suffered or permitted to work[75]—is considered work time and is compensable. Modifications like these may be unlawful under the FLSA.

One of the most common lawsuits is the wage and hour lawsuit, in which employees claim that employers have not paid them for all hours worked or for owed overtime. Employers found liable may be required to pay damages, including back pay, attorney fees, and civil or criminal penalties under both federal and state laws. Employers may also be held personally liable under the FLSA. The FLSA defines an employer as "any person acting directly or indirectly in the interest of an employer in relation to an employee."[76]

An employer may want to take measures to minimize time record changes, including requiring all employees to record and maintain their own time records. Supervisors may also record or closely monitor hours worked. Employers should hold employees accountable to timekeeping policies and procedures.

Employers may want to prohibit changes to time records unless preapproved, develop policies prohibiting off-the-clock work, ensure employees are relieved of all duties during meal periods, have employees sign and date their own time records, and require employees and employers to acknowledge when changes are made to a time record.

When changes are made to a time record, an employer may want to keep the original record and create a modified record, or line through the error on the original time record, make the correction, and have both the employer and employee sign and date. Documentation should be established to note the reason for any changes. Automated timekeeping systems typically have features to record a history of changes and who made them. These systems may also be set up to obtain the acknowledgment of both the employee and the employer when changes occur.

To minimize liability, timekeeping records should be maintained in such a way that a third party, such as an auditor from the DOL, can tell that the records, including any changes, are genuine and reflect the time actually worked

Q: A company participates in an annual trade show held on a weekend. Is it acceptable to allow employees to volunteer to work at the trade show booth?

The short answer is no. In for-profit, private-sector organizations, employers are unlikely to have unpaid workers. Generally speaking, all employees must be paid at least the minimum wage. However, some categories of employers may receive volunteer services under certain circumstances. For example, in government and nonprofit organizations, volunteers may exist.

Volunteers are typically engaged in activity for a public service, charitable, or religious organization. The DOL's "FLSA Advisor" on volunteers explains:[77]

> Individuals who volunteer or donate their services, usually on a part-time basis, for public service, religious, or humanitarian objectives, not as employees and without contemplation of pay, are not considered employees of the religious, charitable, or similar non-profit organizations that receive their service.

> For example, members of civic organizations may help out in a sheltered workshop; men's or women's organizations may send members or students into hospitals or nursing homes to provide certain personal services for the sick or elderly; parents may assist in a school library or cafeteria as a public duty to maintain effective services for their children or they may volunteer to drive a school bus to carry a football team or school band on a trip. Similarly, an individual may volunteer to perform such tasks as driving vehicles or folding bandages for the Red Cross, working with disabled children or disadvantaged youth, helping in youth programs as camp counselors, scoutmasters, den mothers, providing child care assistance for needy working mothers, soliciting contributions or participating in benefit programs for such organizations, and volunteering other services needed to carry out their charitable, educational, or religious programs.

In the vast majority of circumstances, individuals can volunteer services to public-sector employers.[78] When Congress amended the FLSA in 1985, it made clear that people are allowed to volunteer their services to public agencies and their community with but one exception—public-sector employers may not allow their employees to volunteer,[79] without compensation, additional time to do the same work for which they are employed. There is no prohibition on anyone employed in the private sector from volunteering in any capacity or line of work in the public sector.

Q: May an employer deduct a half day from an exempt employee's pay when he or she is out half a day due to personal reasons and has exhausted all paid time off?
Partial-day wage deductions from exempt employees' pay are often confusing situations for employers.

Permissible deductions from the fixed weekly salary of exempt employees are described under 29 C.F.R. Section 541.602.[80] In nearly all cases, deductions of salary for exempt employees are allowed only in full-day increments.[81] If an exempt employee is absent two full days for personal reasons, the employer may deduct two full day's pay. If the employee is absent for one-and-a-half days, the employer may deduct only for one full day. No pay is required for any workweek in which the employee performs no work. This is true for sick leave as well, though certain exceptions do apply under the Family and Medical Leave Act (FMLA).

The requirement to pay the full day's salary to the exempt employee for a partial-day absence is the same for employers who have a bona fide leave plan as well as for those without a leave plan, and it applies to the private sector only; there are exclusions for the public sector.

To summarize, partial-day deductions from exempt employees'

pay are allowed only in the following situations:

- For violations of safety rules of major significance. Safety rules of major significance include those related to prevention of serious workplace dangers, such as rules banning smoking in explosive plants, oil refineries, and coal mines.
- For partial-day absences specifically mandated under the FMLA.
- In the first and last weeks of employment.

Q: May an employer make deductions from an exempt employee's pay for a holiday he or she is not yet eligible for?

Though there is no requirement that an employer must provide paid holidays to employees, when employers do make deductions from an exempt employee's salary, they need to ensure that they are not violating the FLSA's salary basis requirement.[82] Violations of the salary basis test can cause employees to lose their exempt status. Making a deduction from an exempt employee's salary for a holiday when the company is closed would likely violate the FLSA salary basis requirement.

To qualify as exempt from the FLSA's overtime requirements, employees must have certain job duties and must be paid on a salary basis. Salary basis is defined as the payment on a weekly or less frequent basis of a predetermined amount that constitutes all or part of compensation, without reductions for variations in the quality or quantity of the work performed. Only limited salary deductions are permitted for time missed without jeopardizing employees' exempt status.

According to Section 541.118 of the FLSA regulations,

"An employee will not be considered to be 'on a salary basis' if deductions from his predetermined compensation are made for absences occasioned by the employer or by the operating requirements of the business. Accordingly, if the employee is ready, willing, and able to work, deductions may not be made for time when work is not available."[83]

Because the company holiday is an "absence occasioned by the employer," and the employer has no way of knowing whether the employee would be "ready, willing, and able to work" on that day, reducing the employee's pay for the holiday could violate the salary basis test.

The FLSA permits employers to reduce a salaried, exempt employee's pay for a workweek only in the following situations:

- The employee missed one or more full days for personal reasons other than illness or accident.
- The employee was absent for one or more full days because of illness or accident, and you reduce the salary according to a bona fide sickness/accident plan, policy, or practice.
- The employee received compensation for serving in the military or on jury duty, and you reduce the employee's regular salary by that amount.
- The employee broke a major safety rule, and you reduce the employee's salary as a good-faith penalty.
- The employee received an unpaid disciplinary suspension of one or more full days imposed in good faith for infractions of workplace conduct rules.
- The employee was absent for an entire workweek (exempt employees do not have to be paid for any workweek in which they perform no work).
- The employee did not work some days during the first or last week of employment.

- The employee took intermittent leave under the FMLA.

The FLSA regulations do not specifically allow deductions for holidays. Therefore, employers should not make deductions from an exempt employee's pay for holidays, lest they risk losing the employee's exempt status.

Q: What are an employer's obligations relative to pay when the company must close early due to inclement weather?

Whether facing a threat of hurricanes along the Gulf Coast, or a blizzard in Buffalo, closing a business because of inclement weather can cause more than just logistical headaches. Federal[84] and state[85] laws govern how employees should be paid under these circumstances, and employers must take care to ensure compliance with the laws. With knowledge, preparation, and communication regarding pay-related matters and unexpected closures, both employers and employees will understand the reasons a company will or will not pay employees in the event of weather-related closures.

The easiest class of employee to address is the nonexempt, or hourly, employee. Under the FLSA, employers are only required to pay nonexempt employees for actual hours in which they perform work. Under the FLSA, an employer is not obligated to pay a nonexempt employee for time in which he or she performs no work, even if the employee was scheduled to work and was sent home early. This means that if a business decides to shut down and sends employees home in the middle of the shift, the employer is permitted to pay nonexempt employees only for the time spent working.

However, to complicate matters, some states have enacted "report-in pay" laws.[86] These laws are established to provide some guaranteed pay for nonexempt employees who go through the trouble and expense of coming to work, only to be sent home. Employers, particularly multistate employers, must ensure that they are familiar with the state laws regarding report-in pay. If such a state law exists, then employers must comply, and they may be required to pay for a certain number of hours, even if not worked.

The aspect of inclement weather closings and pay that causes employers the most headaches is how to handle pay for exempt employees. The solution is simple. Exempt employees must almost always be paid. The FLSA has an exclusive list of the instances in which an employer is permitted to dock exempt employee pay, and business closures are not one of the permitted deductions.[87] If an employer sends exempt employees home because of inclement weather, an employer is obligated to pay them for the entire day under federal law. If an employer decides to close for an entire day because of inclement weather, an employer is still required to pay the exempt employee for the entire day. The only instance in which an employer is permitted to not pay an exempt employee because of inclement weather is when a business closes for an entire week, and exempt employees perform no work during that week.

Although an employer is required to pay exempt employees for most inclement weather closures, an employer is permitted to require exempt employees to use their paid time off. However, if the exempt employee does not have enough paid leave to cover the absence, the employer is not permitted to deduct the difference from the exempt employee's salary. The best way to handle this situation is to include language that explains instances in which employees may be required to use paid leave in the company handbook.

Businesses should also determine how they will handle instances in which the use of paid leave is required but the exempt employee does not have enough leave to cover the absence. For example, a company policy could require an exempt employee to deduct future leave to cover the hours, or the company could choose to advance the employee leave and not deduct the hours from the exempt employee's leave bank.

An effective practice is to communicate this policy to all affected employees whenever there is a threat of inclement weather. Whatever the forecast, knowing your legal obligations and communicating your practices to employees in advance can go a long way to ensure bad weather closures are handled as smoothly as possible.

Q: What are the consequences of making an illegal deduction from an exempt employee's pay?

An employer may rectify improper pay without penalty as long as the employer follows the FLSA "safe harbor" rules.[88]

Under the old FLSA regulations, if the employer made improper deductions to an exempt employee's pay, that employee and all other exempt employees in the same job classification would lose exempt status for that pay period. Consequently, the employer would have to pay that employee and all others in the same class any overtime pay they would have earned if they were nonexempt.

Under more recent FLSA rules, if the employer makes an improper deduction to an exempt employee's salary but follows the FLSA safe harbor provisions, the employer is required to correct the pay of the employee, but the employee and all other employees in the same class will not lose their exempt status for that pay period.

The rules permit employers to protect themselves under the safe harbor provision by doing the following:

- Establishing a clearly communicated policy prohibiting improper deductions and including a complaint mechanism.
- Reimbursing employees for any improper deductions in a reasonable time frame.
- Making a good-faith commitment to comply in the future.

Employers are free to distribute this policy in written form either directly to the employee or through the employee handbook or organization intranet. If the employer follows safe harbor rules, the FLSA provides a window of time in which the employer may correct the employee's pay, and the employer will not lose the exemption for an entire class of employees, as long as the improper calculation to the single employee's pay was isolated or inadvertent.

If an employer willfully violates the policy, for example, by continuing the improper deductions after receiving employee complaints, or has an "actual practice" of making improper deductions, the employer could jeopardize the exempt status of an entire class and might be required to pay all hours plus overtime pay to those affected. To determine whether an employer has such a practice, relevant factors include the following:

- The number of improper deductions.
- The time frame.
- The number and geographic location of employees and managers in charge.
- Whether the employer has a clearly communicated policy prohibiting improper deductions.

Understanding the law and making a good-faith effort to comply with FLSA requirements are not enough. Employers should at a minimum establish a safe harbor policy to limit the liability associated with isolated and inadvertent deductions. Refer to the FLSA regulation that applies to safe harbor policies.[89]

Q: May an employer require that exempt employees use their paid time off during a business closure of less than a week? If not, is it permissible to deduct from the exempt employees' pay for the time not worked?

Although private employers are not required under most state laws[90] or the FLSA to provide PTO for their employees, generally, employers that do provide PTO may require employees to apply this time off to specific days, as designated by the employer. This mandatory use of PTO can be applied to full- or partial-day absences, as long as the exempt employees' salaries are not affected. During mandatory partial or full workweek business closures for holidays, vacations, and other breaks from work, employers may require that exempt employees use their accrued and available PTO to cover their absences. This requirement can be applied to situations in which the business is closed for either a full or partial workweek without affecting the employees' exempt statuses.[91]

However, according to a DOL Opinion Letter,[92] exempt employees who are required by policy to use their PTO for absences occasioned by the employer or by the operating requirements of the business must still receive their guaranteed salaries for closures of less than a full workweek, even if they have exhausted their available leave, have insufficient accrued leave, or have a negative leave balance. An exempt employee is paid on a salary basis, which means that the employee regularly receives a predetermined or guaranteed salary that is not subject to reduction, despite the number of days or hours worked in a workweek. An exempt employee may not be subject to a wage deduction for full- or partial-day absences based on business closures occasioned by the employer or by the operating requirements of the business. If an exempt employee is ready, willing, and able to work, an employer may not make wage deductions for time not worked during a workweek when work is not available. However, if an exempt employee performs no work for the entire workweek of a business closure, then the exempt employee is not required to be paid for that week, and the exempt status of the employee will not be violated.

When requiring employees to use their PTO for mandatory business closures, employers should have a written policy in place to inform employees of this requirement. Policies should be applied fairly and consistently to avoid any potential discriminatory claims from employees. Employers will also want to ensure that their policy on mandatory use of PTO during business closures is in compliance with their states' laws.

Q: Under the FLSA, may an employer dock an employee's pay as a disciplinary penalty?

Although it is discouraged by many experts, employers may in some circumstances dock pay to penalize an employee for violating a written policy.

An employer cannot refuse to pay a nonexempt worker for hours that the employee has worked, but the FLSA does not prohibit employers from reducing a nonexempt worker's hourly wage rate as a disciplinary action. Nonexempt employees must only be paid the minimum wage.

Therefore, unless a union contract or other employment agreement provides otherwise, under federal law employers are entitled to reduce pay of nonexempt workers, as long as the workers are still are paid the minimum wage. Employers may not dock the pay of a minimum-wage earner for violating a policy or committing a safety infraction.

Exempt employees are usually paid salaries, and any reduction to those salaries must comply with the FLSA regulations—otherwise, the employees' exempt status will be jeopardized. Under 29 C.F.R. Section 541.602, deductions from exempt employees' pay can be taken for disciplinary suspensions, but they must be made on a full-day basis only.[93] In addition, the suspension must be imposed as a result of a serious violation of workplace conduct rules, such as engaging in dangerous behavior in the workplace or committing sexual harassment. The DOL excludes suspensions related to performance issues and poor attendance from the definition of "violations of workplace conduct rules." Finally, according to the regulations, the suspension must be part of a "written policy applicable to all employees."

Courts interpreting the FLSA rules, however, have ruled that if an employer routinely makes salary deductions of less than a full week for disciplinary reasons or has an employment policy that creates a significant likelihood of such deductions, the salary requirement is not satisfied and the employee is not exempt from the FLSA.[94]

Q: When a company hires or terminates an exempt worker midweek, must that worker be paid for the entire week?

An employer is not obligated to pay an exempt worker's full salary when the employee works only a partial workweek during his or her first or last workweek of employment.

Under the FLSA, workers must meet certain tests regarding their job duties and must usually be paid on a salary basis to be exempt from minimum wage and overtime requirements. The salary-basis test requires that the employee receive a salary of no less than $455 per week. (Check your state laws for states with a higher minimum salary threshold.)

However, the FLSA regulations state in 29 C.F.R. Section 541.602,

> "An employer is not required to pay the full salary in the initial or terminal week of employment. Rather, an employer may pay a proportionate part of an employee's full salary for the time actually worked in the first and last week of employment. In such weeks, the payment of an hourly or daily

> equivalent of the employee's full salary for the time
> actually worked will meet the requirement."[95]

During the first and last weeks of employment, an employer may pay an exempt worker an amount that is proportional to the amount of time actually worked. Payment on a daily or hourly basis proportionally equivalent to the employee's salary is acceptable.

This exception to the salary basis test does not apply to a worker who is employed for only a few days. Casual or occasional employment is not consistent with employment on a salary basis. As a result, an employee who works only a few days would not be regarded as exempt and should be paid at least minimum wage and overtime.

Q: What are the FLSA guidelines for employing young workers?

The FLSA is the federal law that restricts the employment of youth in the workplace. Regulations are designed to protect the educational opportunities of youth and prohibit their employment in jobs that are detrimental to their health and safety. The FLSA provides age and wage requirements and work hours restrictions and lists hazardous occupations too dangerous for young workers to perform. There are a number of exemptions[96] to the federal youth labor laws. In addition, many states have laws related to the employment of minors. If the state law[97] and the federal law overlap, the law that offers more protections to the minor will apply.

Age Requirements

The minimum age for most nonagricultural work under the FLSA is 14. However, at any age, young workers may deliver newspapers; perform in radio, television, movie, or theatrical productions; work in businesses owned by their parents (except in mining, manufacturing, or hazardous jobs[98]); and perform babysitting or minor chores around a private home. Also, at any age, youth may be employed as homeworkers to gather evergreens and make evergreen wreaths. The federal law contains a number of requirements that apply only to particular types of jobs (for example, agricultural work,[99] operation of motor vehicles,[100] and work by a minor for his or her parents[101]).

Work Hours

The FLSA does not limit the number of hours or times of day for workers 16 years of age and older.

Hours worked by 14- and 15-year-olds are limited to the following:

- Nonschool hours.
- Three hours in a school day.
- Eighteen hours in a school week.
- Eight hours in a nonschool day.
- Forty hours in a nonschool week.
- Hours between 7:00 a.m. and 7:00 p.m. (except from June 1 through Labor Day, when evening hours are extended to 9:00 p.m.)
- 14- and 15-year-old workers enrolled in an approved Work Experience and Career Exploration Program (WECEP)[102] may be employed for up to twenty-three hours in a school week and three hours on school days (including during school hours).

Wages

An employer is permitted to pay employees under age 20 a minimum wage equal to $4.25 per hour for the first 90 days of employment if the youth's employment does not displace other workers.[103]

Safety and Health

The FLSA generally prohibits minors under 18 years of age from work in any occupation deemed to be hazardous by the Secretary of Labor.[104] Among these occupations are excavation, manufacturing explosives, mining, and operating many types of power-driven equipment.

Work Permits and Age Certificates

No federal laws require work permits or age certificates for minors to be employed. However, many states require them.[105] The DOL will issue an age certificate if the minor employee's state does not issue it, or if the minor is requested by his or her employer to provide one.

Additional Resources

FLSA—Child Labor Rules Advisor[106]
FLSA Regulations
Hazardous Farm Work Regulation[107]
Age Requirements[108]

Chapter 7
Paid Leave Benefits
(Paid Time Off and Sick Time)

Q: Must employees on military leave be paid? Can they be required to use paid time off or vacation time for their military service?

The Uniformed Services Employment and Reemployment Rights Act (USERRA)[1] protects from discrimination or retaliation an employee who gives proper notice of the need for a military-related absence and provides job reinstatement rights for up to five years. There is no requirement under USERRA to pay the employee for the military-related absence. In addition, an employer is prohibited from requiring the employee to use his or her paid time-off benefits for the military absence; however, the employer must allow the use of paid time off if the employee requests it.

This concept is fairly straightforward when it comes to nonexempt hourly employees as these employees need only be paid for the hours they work. But how does military leave affect an exempt, salaried employee? Deductions for partial-week absences due to military leave are prohibited under the Fair Labor Standards Act (FLSA) (29 C.F.R. Section 541.602).[2] If an exempt employee works any portion of the workweek, the employer must pay the employee his or her full weekly salary as if he or she had worked the entire week. According to the salary basis,

> "While an employer cannot make deductions
> from pay for absences of an exempt employee occa-
> sioned by . . . temporary military leave, the employer

can offset any amounts received by an employee as . . . military pay for a particular week against the salary due for that particular week without loss of the exemption."[3]

In other words, the salary cannot be reduced because of military leave, but the employer is allowed to offset amounts received by the employee as military pay.

Again, the employer cannot require employees to use their paid time-off benefits for the absence, so employers may have to pay exempt employees for hours not worked without charging their leave bank.

Some states have additional military leave laws that may be more generous than USERRA, and employers are encouraged to check their state law when encountered with a request for military leave.

Q: Are employers required to pay out unused vacation pay to employees who leave the company?

Accrued vacation is normally paid to employees who are leaving the company regardless of the reason for separation. Some companies may also pay terminating employees prorated vacation pay for any vacation time that they would have earned during the next year, provided they have met all the necessary eligibility requirements under the employer's policy. Although employers may place certain restrictions on vacation pay rights, many states have state law provisions that require an employer to pay any accrued vacation pay upon termination of employment with the company. In many other states, vacation pay is included in the definition of "wages" in the state's wage and hour laws, also making it a requirement that employers pay terminating employees for this time. It is always advisable to check individual state laws on payment of final wages to assure compliance, and to avoid any penalties and fines. A state law guide such as the *State by State Guide to Human Resources Law* can serve as a practical resource.[4]

Chapter 8
Payroll

Q: What is a company's obligation in terms of holiday pay for employees working compressed workweeks?

How a company handles holiday pay in response to a compressed workweek is a matter of internal policy. Employers typically establish specific holiday pay practices for employees on compressed workweek schedules. The employee should normally receive the same amount—not more, not less—of paid holiday time off as employees on regular schedules. To accomplish that, employees on compressed work schedules are often required to work the additional hours or use personal leave to make up the difference between their regular work schedule and the holiday hours paid. For example, if an employee works 10-hour shifts and the employer's policy is to pay eight hours of holiday pay, the employee would be required to make up the additional two hours of missed work time on another day.

In most cases, when the holiday falls on a scheduled day off, the employee has already worked a full workweek and would not be entitled to any additional pay for the holiday. Some employers allow employees to apply a floating holiday's pay to that situation, permit employees to take holiday leave on an alternate day, or otherwise credit the holiday time toward the employee's weekly hours.

Q: How should an employer handle a final paycheck, taxes, and benefits for a recently deceased employee?

First, confirm the state law[1] regarding final pay for deceased employees. As a general rule, an uncashed paycheck issued prior to the employee's death should be canceled, and a new check should be issued in the name of the employee's estate or beneficiary. The new check should have the same amount withheld for tax purposes as the old check.

In the likely event wages are still owed the employee at the time of death, issue a check made to the beneficiary or to the estate of the employee. Final wages paid within the same calendar year in which the employee died are not subject to Federal Income Tax Withholdings (FITW),[2] but they are subject to taxes under the Federal Insurance Contributions Act (FICA)[3] and the Federal Unemployment Tax Act (FUTA).[4]

If the wages are paid in the year following the employee's death, they are not subject to FITW, FICA, or FUTA taxes.

Next, locate beneficiary designations for all benefits as quickly as possible. Schedule a time to meet with the beneficiaries, if possible, to discuss the benefits that the beneficiaries are eligible to receive and the process for administering the claims.

Third, treat accrued but unused vacation, sick, paid time off (PTO), and other leave in accordance with your state law.[5] If no law exists, follow organizational policy.

The next step is to terminate health insurance according to the policy as of date of death. If applicable, determine the balance of the health care flexible spending account for health expenses prior to date of death, and notify the family about the process to access these funds. If the employee had a spouse or dependents enrolled in the medical plan, notify these individuals of the option to continue their coverage under COBRA.[6]

Finally, follow normal termination checklist procedures to ensure the return of all equipment, keys, credit cards, and other items and to address security issues.

Q: What issues should a company be concerned about before deciding to change its payroll frequency?

First consider state wage payment provisions. Each state dictates wage payment frequency.

Overtime

How will the change and corresponding transition affect overtime? Fair Labor Standards Act (FLSA) regulations indicate that employees who have been classified as nonexempt are required to be paid overtime when they work more than 40 hours in a workweek.[7] The regulations also define the workweek as "a fixed and regularly recurring period of 168 hours—seven consecutive 24-hour periods. It need not coincide with the calendar week but may begin on any day and at any hour of the day."[8] Verify that changing your payday does not have the unintended consequence of inadvertently placing your organization into an overtime situation. If so, will the temporary cost be worth it in the long term?

Direct Deposits

If your organization offers direct deposit of employee paychecks, you will need to coordinate with the various financial institutions to ensure timely and accurate deposits, especially during the transition. Instituting a direct deposit program involves an employer establishing a direct deposit date similar to a "pay day" with both the employer's financial institution or payroll service provider and employees' financial institutions. On the direct deposit date, funds from the employer's financial institution need to be electronically deposited into employees' accounts at the employees' receiving financial institutions. Many direct deposits are done through a process known as Automated Clearing House, which allows for the secure transfer of funds approximately one to two days prior to the direct deposit date.[9]

Pay Day Traditions

Pay day traditions, such as providing free coffee and donuts, longer lunch hours for employees to deposit their paychecks, special office hours reserved for field personnel to collect their paychecks, or the CEO's hand delivery of them, may have evolved in your organization. You may need to take into account how cherished traditions could be affected by a change in pay days.

Communication and Education

Proactive and frequent communication throughout the organization is vitally important in any change initiative and especially when changing pay days. Do not limit communication and educational efforts to displaying posters, sending e-mails, or placing notices on organization bulletin boards and the intranet. Try new approaches such as hosting a new pay day fair. Invite your payroll processor or other vendors to participate. Use this fair as an opportunity to educate your employees about direct deposit or other alternative paycheck options, the organization's 401(k), and other financial planning or credit counseling resources.

Q: Can an employer ask to see the Social Security card of new hires for payroll purposes?

According to the Internal Revenue Service (IRS), the answer is yes. The IRS "Hiring Employees" guidance reads:

> You are required to get each employee's name and Social Security Number (SSN) and to enter them on Form W-2. (This requirement also applies to resident and nonresident alien employees.) You should ask your employee to show you his or her social security card. The employee may show the card if it is available. You may, but are not required to, photocopy

the social security card if the employee provides it. Record each new employee's name and social security number from his or her social security card.[10]

Do not confuse this requirement with I-9 requirements.[11] Employers cannot require an employee to produce specific documents for I-9 purposes. But you can ask specifically to see a Social Security card for payroll purposes separately from when the employee completes the I-9 form. If a new hire does not have a social security card, he or she should be directed to the Social Security Administration to request a replacement card or to apply for a new card.[12]

Q: How should a company process pay for an employee who was hired, worked for three days, and then was terminated?

Employers must pay all employees for work performed, even though it may be a challenge paying an employee who has not provided proper documentation.

According to Department of Labor (DOL) Fact Sheet #22,

> "Work not requested but suffered or permitted
> to be performed is work time that must be paid for
> by the employer. . . . The reason is immaterial. The
> hours are work time and are compensable."[13]

The IRS expects employers to withhold payroll taxes from employees, regardless of their I-9 status.[14]

Here are some tips to follow to ensure there is no violation of the FLSA or IRS rules:

- **Pay.** To satisfy both the DOL's requirement and the IRS's expectation of the employer, the employer must pay the employee and ensure that the appropriate taxes are paid to the IRS by paying the employee his or her wages owed in cash, less the amount deducted for taxes, or by generating a check within the company payroll system, less the amount deducted for taxes.

- **Plan.** Employers should have all paperwork for new employees completed as soon as possible before any other work is performed. No work should be permitted until the employee has completed the I-9 and presented the requisite documents, and payroll has a copy of the employee's Social Security card.

Careful planning and a well-executed process for hiring will save employers time and trouble in the long run.

Q: How should a company handle uncashed paychecks by current or former employees?

The answer to this question falls into the "unclaimed property law" arena. All 50 states have provisions regarding how to treat "unclaimed property." The provisions are similar in one regard— how to determine if the property, in this case the paycheck, is abandoned and when to report this information to the state.

There are four elements to consider:

- Does the property have value?
- Can the owner of the paycheck be located?
- Has the paycheck been unclaimed for the period of time set by the state law or the "abandonment period?" An employer will want to check with the state law regarding the length of time the paycheck needs to be "abandoned."
- Is there a legal obligation of the "holder" (employer) to the "owner" (employee)?

Employers should create policies and procedures for handling unclaimed wages or paychecks. Some items to include in the policies and procedures are the following:

- Try to make contact with the employee or former employee by phone to discuss the paycheck(s) that was not cashed. Document any attempts your company has made to have the person collect his or her wages. An employer will need to show that the employee/former employee could not be located.
- When phone attempts do not work, written notice should go to the employee's last known address (or addresses); use certified mail, or have some sort of record of attempt.
- Check state regulations regarding unclaimed property to find out the "abandonment period." Keep in mind that all 50 states as well as the District of Columbia have different regulations, so it is important to double-check.
- Once the "abandonment period" passes, file and report the unclaimed property with the appropriate state authorities.

Employers should know that most states have increased enforcement of unclaimed property laws over the years. They have also increased the size of the unclaimed property offices (including the number of auditors), the number of audits done, and the educational programs dealing with this topic.

Employers are required to turn over unclaimed wages to the state.

Q: Should an employer pay accrued vacation leave at the rate of pay the employee actually earned the leave or at his or her current rate of pay?

The rate of vacation payout is generally governed by the employer as long as it meets federal or state minimum wage requirements. For administrative ease, many employers choose to pay out accrued vacation leave at the employee's current rate of pay. However, employers should check state legal requirements to ensure there is no additional legal obligation. California, for example, requires employers to pay leave at the employee's current rate of pay.

In contrast, the employer may also choose to pay out vacation leave at the earned rate of pay rather than at the current rate of pay. For example, the employee may have earned vacation leave last year, when his or her wage was $10.00 per hour, but his or her current wage is $12.00 per hour. An employer may choose to pay out the vacation leave at the earned rate of $10.00 per hour. In this case, an employer should consider a few points. First, the employer will need to have an established policy that informs employees of all rules regarding paid vacation leave, including payment of vacation hours. Second, the employer should develop a detailed process to track each employee's accrued vacation time and the rate at which it is earned. This process can result in a complicated system that requires close monitoring when calculating and tracking different rates of pay. Additionally, an employer must ensure that the payout policy is administered consistently to all employees. Finally, an employer will need to determine the most ethical way to address the payment of vacation leave based on the organization's culture, values, and future goals.

Employers may also impose restrictions and other conditions regarding vacation payout, and these restrictions should be communicated to employees at the time they begin work. (In a number of states, this communication is required.) A growing body of state laws and court decisions govern how employers administer vacation time, including payout at termination for accrued but unused vacation. Employers should carefully review their state laws[15] to develop a comprehensive policy covering leave eligibility, accrual, carryover, forfeiture, payment at termination, and integration of vacation policy with other state laws.

Q: Can an employer hold a terminated employee's final paycheck until company equipment is returned, or deduct the cost from the final pay?

Employers cannot withhold an employee's paycheck until equipment is returned. On a federal level, the FLSA mandates that wages are due on the next regular payday for the covered pay period, and several states have clear provisions that an employee must receive payment upon termination. Neither of these allows for any exceptions related to unreturned equipment; therefore, pay cannot be withheld past these requirements.

An employer might be able to deduct the cost of the equipment from the final pay. The specific circumstances of the situation and state wage deduction laws will determine whether an employer may do this. Generally speaking, state wage deduction laws allow employers to deduct monies from an employee's pay required by law (such as federal and state taxes and Social Security), benefit deductions, or deductions ordered by a court or collective bargaining agreement. In some states, the wage deduction laws allows an employer to make other deductions if the employer has written authorization from the employee. If the employee works in a state that does not prohibit this type of deduction, then the employer may withhold the cost of the item from the employee's pay with the written authorization.

However, there are some states, like California, that—even with written authorization from an employee—have additional restrictions that the employer must follow.

If an employer reviews state wage deduction and wage payment laws to find it cannot deduct from pay, the employer might consider invoicing the employee for cost of the equipment, or pursuing the matter by taking the former employee to small claims court to receive a legal judgment against that person for the cost of the item.

Q: Can a company hold a paycheck from employees because they did not turn in their timesheet? If not, how can the employee be disciplined?

Wage payment laws require employers to pay their employees for all hours worked on regularly scheduled paydays set by the employer. Failure to turn in a timesheet does not warrant an exception to these laws. Employers may argue that they cannot pay the employee without the timesheet because they do not know what hours the employee worked. However, under the FLSA, the employer's obligation is to keep record of the hours worked by employees, and though many employers rely on employees' assistance via a timesheet or time clock, the employer is ultimately responsible.[16] Therefore, the employer must pay the employee for all hours worked, regardless of whether the employee recorded his or her time or turned this information in to the employer.

So, how can the employer ensure that it pays the employee correctly? Ultimately, it may come down to contacting the employee for an accounting of his or her hours verbally or paying the employee for the hours he or she was scheduled to work. In addition, an employer should establish clear timekeeping guidelines and procedures, whether they involve a time clock, paper-and-pencil timesheets, or computer-based time-tracking programs, and discipline employees accordingly for failure to follow these procedures. Any discipline that is consistently applied without discrimination and that does not involve withholding pay for time worked is appropriate. If you have a progressive discipline policy, follow those procedures as you would for any other policy or procedure violation in the workplace.

Chapter 9
Planning & Design

Q: What are the advantages or disadvantages of a lead, match, or lag compensation strategy?

When developing an internal compensation structure, an organization needs to determine how it wishes its rates of pay to compare to the rates of pay in the relative marketplace. Organizations have several options when implementing a compensation strategy:

- Match the market by paying rates comparable to those of the relative marketplace.
- Lead the market by paying rates that are higher than the relative marketplace.
- Lag the market by paying rates lower than those of the relative marketplace.
- Use a combination of the preceding three options.

Match the Market

One of the most common compensation strategies for many employers is to set pay levels relative to those in the existing marketplace. By matching the pay rates of its competitors, the organization ensures its compensation structure remains competitive, therefore improving its ability to attract and retain top talent. Although this strategy allows employers to better manage labor costs, it also has the potential of placing the employer in a position of having to play catch-up, requiring larger adjustments to the compensation structure during tight labor markets.

Lead the Market

An employer may choose to establish an internal compensation strategy that is in excess of the pay rates in the prevailing marketplace. This compensation strategy may increase the supply of candidates, improve selection rates of qualified applicants, decrease employee turnover, boost morale and productivity, or prevent unionization efforts. However, prior to implementing a lead compensation strategy, an organization should carefully consider what benefits it expects to realize from such a strategy, keeping in mind that this type of structure has the greatest propensity of increasing overall labor costs. This strategy may be most appropriate for organizations located in highly competitive labor markets that want to ensure their pay rates are continuously equal to the marketplace. Employers that adopt such a strategy will need to monitor it closely to determine whether the anticipated benefits of the strategy are being realized.

Lag the Market

An employer may choose to establish an internal compensation strategy that pays less than the marketplace. This is probably the least recommended strategy. Organizations that choose to implement a compensation strategy that lags the marketplace may do so because they simply do not have the financial resources to pay higher rates. These employers may attempt to reward employees in nonmonetary ways to minimize dissatisfaction and turnover.

Unfortunately, organizations that choose or are forced to set pay rates below the prevailing marketplace are much more susceptible to fluctuations in the labor market, risk greater difficulty in retaining and attracting highly qualified candidates, and typically tend to experience higher rates of employee dissatisfaction, poor performance, and turnover.

Combination of Options

For other organizations, a combination of any of the three options may be most appropriate. For example, an employer may choose to lead the market during tight labor markets. This method requires closer monitoring, and pay rates will need to be adjusted throughout the year.

Regardless of which option an organization ultimately adopts, the compensation strategy will set forth the organization's philosophy regarding internal pay rates relative to the rates of pay in the marketplace. There is no one best compensation strategy, and which strategy is appropriate for a particular organization cannot be answered in the abstract. However, an organization's compensation strategy should match the particular circumstances of each organization's mission, vision, and culture and support the organization's overall business strategy.

Q: What should be included in a compensation philosophy?

A compensation philosophy is simply a formal statement documenting the company's position about employee compensation. It essentially explains the "why" behind employee pay and creates a framework for consistency. Employers can benefit from being transparent about their compensation philosophy and having an official pay strategy.

Compensation philosophies are typically developed by the HR department in collaboration with the executive team. The philosophy is based on many factors, including the company's financial position, the size of the organization, the industry, business objectives, salary survey information, and the level of difficulty in finding qualified talent based on the economy, as well as the unique circumstances of the business. The compensation philosophy should be reviewed periodically and modified based on how well it is working and on current factors affecting the business. For example, market conditions may make it difficult to find qualified talent in a particular specialization, and an employer may need to pay a premium for these candidates. If the employer's current compensation philosophy does not support this value, then the organization may need to change its philosophy to meet its current needs.

A well-designed compensation philosophy supports the organization's strategic plan and initiatives, business goals, competitive outlook, operating objectives, and compensation and total reward strategies.

As such, most compensation philosophies seek to do the following:

- Identify the organization's pay programs and total reward strategies.
- Identify how the pay programs and strategies support the organization's business strategy, competitive outlook, operating objectives, and human capital needs.
- Attract people to join the organization.
- Motivate employees to perform at the best of their competencies, abilities, and skill sets.
- Retain key talent and reward high-performing employees.
- Define the competitive market position of the organization in relation to base pay, variable compensation, and benefits opportunities.
- Define how the organization plans to pay and reward competitively, based on business conditions, competition, and ability to pay.

An effective compensation philosophy should pass the following quality test:

- Is the overall program equitable?

- Is the overall program defensible and perceived by employees as fair?
- Is the overall program fiscally sensitive?
- Are the programs included in the compensation philosophy and policy legally compliant? Can the organization effectively communicate the philosophy, policy, and overall programs to employees?
- Are the programs the organization offers fair, competitive, and in line with the compensation philosophy and policies?

Though HR is clearly in the lead in developing an organization's compensation philosophy and policy, success lies in close collaboration with the leadership team to obtain valuable input, direction, and concurrence.

Q: What are some common types of differential/premium pay, and in what instances would an employer consider offering this type of pay to its employees?
The Fair Labor Standards Act (FLSA) does not require private employers to provide differential/premium pay to employees, but many employers reward their employees with additional pay in various situations. Employer practices vary widely on this issue. Some reasons for differential pay practices may include shift work, callback work, weekend work, and hazardous or dirty duty.

Shift Differential
The most frequently offered type of differential pay is given for specific work shifts and is common in the manufacturing industry. First-shift hours are considered to be "normal," commonly 7:00 a.m. to 3:00 p.m., and are paid at a "base" rate. Later hours—second and third shifts—are typically less desirable, and as a result,

many employers are able to encourage workers to work these later shifts by providing a higher hourly rate via a differential added to the base rate for hours worked during the less popular shift times. Employers must remember to calculate overtime properly, particularly when the nonexempt employee receives shift differentials in addition to his or her normal hourly base pay rate.[1]

Call-Back Premiums

Call-back premiums are provided for work performed after normal hours, such as during a workplace emergency. The employer might choose to pay a higher hourly rate for call-back hours worked, such as double time (double the hourly rate) or triple time (three times the employee's normal hourly rate). Another way to pay call-back premiums might be to pay the employee for more hours than he or she actually worked or a minimum number of hours. For example, if an employee is called back to work for one hour, the employer might have a policy to provide premium pay of a minimum of two hours, even though the employee did not work two hours. Employers must determine whether the travel time associated with call-back work is compensable under federal and state laws. The FLSA regulation for "Home to Work in Emergency Situations"[2] will help determine whether travel time is compensable, and the Society for Human Resource Management's "Hours of Work"[3] lists state travel time pay provisions.

Weekend and Holiday Premiums

A higher rate of pay is offered for work performed over a weekend or on a company-provided holiday when weekend and holiday work is not part of the employee's regular schedule. For example, work performed on a Saturday might be paid at time and a half while work performed on a Sunday or a holiday might be paid at double an employee's regular hourly rate. Some states[4] have laws requiring premium pay for work performed on weekends or holidays.[5]

Hazard Pay

Hazard pay[6] is often offered when workers are deployed to countries involved in a war or conflict or in situations in which individuals may be directly exposed to hazards on the job (for example, handling explosives). Employee would typically receive the regular rate of pay for their job plus an additional hourly hazard pay rate, although some employers provide hazard pay in the form of lump sum bonuses based on the length of the hazard duty.

Whatever the company practice for differential/premium pay, employers should have a written policy that clearly communicates the amount of additional pay employees receive and under what circumstances.

Q: How does a company establish pay for an employee in an acting or interim role?

Employees may be periodically asked to serve in interim roles or assignments. These assignments may include taking on one or two additional tasks outside the usual scope of work, or assuming the duties of a higher-level position that is vacant.

Many employers have policies that address compensation for employees in interim roles. Although an increase in compensation for an employee may not be required, typical adjustments to compensation include the following:

- A one-time payment or bonus to acknowledge the extra work related to new tasks.
- An increase to base salary for the duration of the interim assignment. For example, if the employee's new role is at the same salary level and involves substantial additional work,

an employer may offer supplemental pay of 5 percent to 15 percent, depending on the nature and amount of the additional work. The amount of supplemental pay may be based on whether the employee functions in both his or her current position as well as in the vacated position, or only in the vacated position.

- An increase to base salary to reflect a higher-level position. If the interim role is at a higher level, the employer may pay the employee a salary appropriate to that position level for the duration of the assignment.

Typically, once an interim assignment ends, the employee's salary returns to the original pay plus any merit increases warranted during this time.

Q: What is the difference between job evaluation and performance evaluation?

There is quite a difference between job and performance evaluations. To avoid confusion, most HR professionals use the phrase "performance appraisal" when discussing the evaluation of an employee's performance on the job.

Job evaluations differ from performance appraisals. Whereas performance appraisals measure employee goals, performance, and outcomes, job evaluation is the process of rank ordering the jobs, not the people, based on job content, to demonstrate the relative worth of all jobs to one another.

Job evaluation takes place early in the process of creating a compensation system for the organization. The content of jobs can be described in terms of factors. Factors are qualities of a job that are common to many kinds of jobs, such as skill, effort, or working conditions. Each factor is assigned a weight, or points, according to how much of that particular factor is present in the job. You may have heard of the "point factor" job evaluation method. Simply stated, the more points assigned to a job, the more worth the job has to the organization. Jobs with more worth are compensated more than jobs with lesser worth.

Ranking the jobs in order of worth after a thorough job evaluation creates a sort of skeleton structure for the assignment of salary ranges. Several good analysis tools for conducting a job evaluation are available, and most compensation consultants have their own favorites that they have developed or used extensively.

Often done by a team of knowledgeable senior employees who understand the functions of most of the jobs in the organization, job evaluation can take several months to complete. Job evaluation is a subjective process, and decisions about which jobs have more worth than others may be personal and somewhat emotional for those involved. If outside consultants lead this effort, they can assist the team in having productive and objective discussions about the various job factors and the weights that should be assigned to them. If the team members know the job incumbents, their personal qualities may be considered as factors instead of the intrinsic factors of the job. When the effort is led by an unbiased outsider who is not acquainted with the job incumbents, there is more perceived fairness to the process.

Q: How does an HR professional create a salary increase matrix for calculating annual merit increases?

First, ask the following questions:

- What is the goal of the company merit increase program?
- Does the organization pay below market, at market, or above market? If you are below market, do you want to make your organization's compensation program more competitive? If

you are at market, do you want to continue the status quo? And if you are above market, are you trying to hold down salary growth?

- What is your organizational philosophy toward excellent performers? What about your substandard performers?

Consider using one of the two approaches outlined below in determining salary increases.

Broadband Approach

If you use a broadband pay structure, you would typically have a percentage increase amount for each level of employee performance regardless of where the employee salary is relative to the midpoint. You would design a spreadsheet with employee ratings on the left side and only one corresponding increase amount for each rating.

You would need to take some initial steps before creating your spreadsheet:

1. Determine the average projected merit increase among organizations for the coming year. Normally, this information becomes available in various surveys in mid-to-late November of each year.
2. Determine your overall salary increase budget.
3. Review your previous year's evaluations to determine a rating distribution. Find the center of distribution (the rating with the most employees). Assuming that this number represents your average employees, this group will receive the median or average increase.
4. Determine the rest of the rating categories (for example, you could use "outstanding," "above average," "below average," and "unsatisfactory").
5. Determine the percentage of total employees in each rating

category. For example, 60 percent of employees are in the average performance rating; 20 percent are above average; 10 percent are outstanding; 5 percent below average; and 5 percent unsatisfactory.

6. Apply that percentage to your total merit increase budget to arrive at the increase distribution for each group.

Or you may simply make an educated guess on the performance distribution:

Performance increase pool amount (total amount available for increases) = 3.5 percent

Ratings with corresponding increase percentages:

Outstanding = 5.5 percent to 6 percent

Above average = 4.5 to 5 percent

Average = 3.5 to 4 percent

Below average = 2 percent

Unsatisfactory = 0

Compa-Ratio Approach

Another way to approach salary increases would be by using a compa-ratio. The first step when using a compa-ratio is to identify where each employee is relative to midpoint. For example, employees with a compa-ratio of 0.80 to 0.89 are below the midpoint of their grade. Therefore, you want to not only reward them based on merit but also provide a higher percentage increase to bring them up in the pay grade. Employees with a compa-ratio of 1.1 to 1.2 are being paid above the grade midpoint. Therefore, their raises will be less. The idea is to provide more internal equity.

On the left side of your spreadsheet, enter the performance level (usually 1 through 5 or "outstanding," "above average," "average," "below average," and "unsatisfactory"). Across the top, enter your compa-ratio segments. For example, you could use 0.8 to 0.89, 0.9 to 0.99, 1.0 to 1.09, and 1.1 to 1.2. Then in the grid below, assign your percentage increases. Very high performers in the 0.8 to 0.89 range would receive the highest increase because they are on the low end of the pay scale compared to their performance, whereas a poor performer in the 1.1 to 1.2 range would receive the least percentage increase because they are on the high end of the pay scale, compared to their performance.

Q: How should salary increases be prorated when an employee's review period is different from the normal time period used for such increases?

Employers typically prorate salary increases for those employees hired since the last focal review date. This practice provides newer employees with a proportionate increase amount compared with other employees. The following are the basic steps in calculating the employees' pay increase appropriate to the period of time they have been employed:

1. Check the terms, and follow the organization's pay increase policy regarding prorating. For example, the policy may have a provision for employees hired midmonth to receive credit for rounding up to the nearest full month.
2. Determine newer employees' expected pay increase amounts that they would have otherwise been entitled to if they had worked the full year.
3. Count the number of months actually worked, and divide it by the number of months under the current increase policy (typically 12 months).
4. Multiply the result by the increase percentage the person would otherwise be entitled to. This is the prorated increase percentage.

Example Calculation

An employee worked six months of the year. The employee would normally receive a 3 percent pay increase had he or she worked the full year.

Six months actually worked divided by 12 months in the review period equals 0.5. Three percent multiplied by 0.5 equals 1.5 percent. The employee in this example would receive a 1.5 percent salary increase.

Q: Can an employer contact other organizations in its area to gauge merit projections or other compensation and benefits data?

This practice may be problematic and could lead to potential risk for employers. Sharing similar information may result in conspiring to fix, maintain, or stabilize benefits for employees by minimizing competition among organizations.

Conducting this type of comparison shopping goes against the provisions of the Sherman Anti-Trust Act of 1890.[7] Congress passed the Sherman Act to protect trade and commerce against unlawful restraints and monopolies. The act prohibits unreasonable restraint of trade to include the potential to set compensation and benefits provided to employees. Based on the power of Congress to regulate interstate commerce, the act declared illegal every contract, combination (in the form of trust or otherwise), or conspiracy in restraint of interstate and foreign trade.

However, employers often want to be competitive in pricing positions; they have a strong desire to know what others are doing. The best practice is to seek resources that have been compiled outside the employer's organization to minimize any evidence supporting antitrust violations. Courts look at intent or reasons behind information sharing. Also considered by courts are the nature, type, timeliness, means, and method of sharing information. Using information secured from a vendor that is in writing, that uses averaged pay rates and aggregate data, that is based on information received from various sources, and that does not directly identify survey participants is in the best interest of the organization.

Q: What are some sources for salary survey data for all industries and occupations?

One of the largest and most comprehensive sources of free salary information is the Bureau of Labor Statistics (BLS).[8] The BLS has salary survey data for many different positions in various industries as well as for specific geographical locations. In addition, the Society for Human Resource Management (SHRM) also has a "Salary Survey Directory" of providers that may sell the survey data.[9] Another opportunity for salary survey information is in the SHRM Compensation Data Center.[10]

Q: What are the benefits of and requirements for establishing a stock option incentive plan?

Incentive stock options (ISOs) provide benefits to both employers and employees. Employers use ISOs as incentives for employees to help make a company profitable. ISOs can be issued by employers on a selective basis and are often provided only to high-income employees.

Employers also use ISOs as a retention tool by attaching a vesting schedule. Vesting generally occurs when the employee completes a specified period of service. Employees who are granted stock options hope to profit by buying stock at the stated option price instead of at the higher market price. Employees may also receive favorable tax treatment. Under the Internal Revenue Code, an employee is not required to include any amount in his or her gross income as a result of the grant or exercise of an option.

However, the employee may be subject to alternative minimum tax in the year he or she exercises the option. When the employee chooses to sell the stock received by exercising the option, the employee will gain taxable income or incur a deductible loss. This amount is generally treated as a capital gain or loss. However, if special holding period requirements are not met, income from the sale must be treated as ordinary income.

To qualify for favorable tax treatment, an ISO must comply with Internal Revenue Service (IRS) requirements. The following are several of the basic statutory requirements:

- The stock option must be an option to purchase stock of the employer corporation or the stock of a parent or subsidiary corporation.
- The option must be granted pursuant to a written agreement that has shareholder approval.
- The option grant must be made within 10 years of establishment of the plan or date of shareholder approval, whichever is earlier.
- The exercise price of an ISO must be no less than the fair market value of the underlying stock on the grant date.
- A plan that permits the grant of ISOs must be approved by shareholders within 12 months of the plan's adoption.

Employers should work closely with their legal counsel and tax advisor to be sure they are complying with applicable IRS regulations and accounting standards.

Q: What are total rewards strategies? How can an HR professional develop total rewards strategies for his or her company?

A total reward strategy is a system implemented by a business that provides monetary, beneficial, and developmental rewards to employees who achieve specific business goals. The strategy combines compensation and benefits with personal growth opportunities inside a motivated work environment.

Designing and implementing a total rewards strategy requires a large-scale approach that drives organizational change. Top executive and management buy-in is critical for the success of a total rewards strategy. Your project team should be made up of decision makers as well as front-line employees to ensure that your approach is well rounded and fits the needs of everyone involved. If you operate in a union environment, collective bargaining may affect the implementation of your strategy.

Developing a total rewards strategy is a four-step process consisting of:

1. **Assessment.** A project team assesses your current benefits and compensation system and determines the effectiveness of those systems in helping your company reach its goals. Activities that take place during the assessment phase of the process include surveying your employees on their opinions and beliefs regarding their pay, benefits, and opportunities for growth and development as well as examining your current policies and practices. The most important outcome of the assessment phase is the project team assessment report, which includes your recommendations for the new total rewards system. The assessment report should include suggested solutions to questions such as the following:

   » Who should be eligible for the rewards?
   » What kinds of behaviors or values are to be rewarded?
   » What type of rewards will work best?
   » How will the company fund the total rewards strategy?

2. **Design.** The senior management team identifies and analyzes various reward strategies to determine what would work best in its workplace. It decides what will be rewarded and what rewards will be offered to employees for those achievements. In a total rewards strategy, pay rewards for achievement of goals will not be the only consideration. HR strategists will also determine additional benefits (flexible work schedule, additional time off) or personal development opportunities (training or promotional) that employees will receive as a result of meeting the established company objectives.

3. **Execution.** The HR department implements the new rewards system. It circulates materials that communicate the new strategy to employees. Training also commences so that managers and decision makers are able to effectively measure the achievement and employees are able to understand what they need to obtain to receive the rewards.

4. **Evaluation.** The effectiveness of the new plan must be measured and the results communicated to company decision makers. Based on the evaluation, modifications can be proposed to the strategy for future implementation.

Chapter 10
Tax Compliance

Q: Are employers required to have employees complete a new W-4 each year?

A W-4 form remains in effect until an employee submits a new one except when an employee claimed to be "exempt from income tax withholding," (not to be confused with the FLSA's use of the term "exempt").

Employers should ensure they have new W-4s for the following employees:

- **New employees.** You should keep copies of the most current W-4s on hand. If the employee needs to change the information later, the employee must fill out a new form, according to the Internal Revenue Service (IRS).
- **Employees who had a change in withholding events during the year.** Events during the year may change an employee's marital status or the exemptions, adjustments, deductions, or credits he or she may expect to claim on return. When this happens, the employee may need to give the employer a new W-4 to change withholding status or number of allowances.
- **Employees claiming exemption from withholding.** To continue to be exempt from withholding in the next year, employees must give employers a new W-4 claiming exempt status by February 15 of that year.

Employers are required to remind employees before December 1 each year to submit a new W-4 form if their withholding allowances have changed or will change for the next year. If the employee does not give the employer a valid W-4 as required, withhold tax as if he or she were single with no withholding allowances, advises the IRS.

Q: What is a 1099-MISC Form, who gets one, and when is it due?

The 1099-MISC Form is an IRS tax return document used to report miscellaneous payments made to nonemployee individuals during the calendar year.[1]

In general, a 1099-MISC Form should be filed for each person to whom you have paid one or more of the following:

- At least $600 in services, rents, prizes or awards, and other income payments.
- At least $10 in royalties or broker payments in lieu of dividends of tax-exempt interest.
- Gross proceeds to an attorney.

Additionally, Form 1099-MISC should be used to report any income from either of the following:

- The result of direct sales of at least $5,000 of consumer products for resale anywhere other than a permanent retail establishment.
- Each person from whom you have withheld federal income tax under the backup withholding rules.

The instructions for Form 1099-MISC provide a comprehensive list of who should and should not receive a form.[2]

There are two major due dates for the Form 1099-MISC. One copy must be sent to each nonemployee individual by January 31.

Another copy must be sent to the IRS by February 28, or if filing electronically, by March 31. Individual states may have varying filing deadlines, so be sure to check with your state.

Information, such as the payer's and the recipient's names, addresses, and federal identification numbers, along with the amount of payments made, must be provided to complete the form.

HR professionals should work closely with their payroll and accounting departments to identify who needs to receive a form. Additionally, employers should consult with their tax professionals and attorneys if they have any concerns about how to calculate income amounts or how to issue the 1099-MISC Form.

Q: If we have employees working in more than one state, what are our state tax withholding obligations?

To determine the specific state obligations for tax withholding, an employer must first understand the tax withholding laws in the states where they conduct business, as well as the laws in the states where employees reside. Consider the following:

- Not all states impose a personal income tax. The states that do not are Alaska, Florida, Nevada, New Hampshire, South Dakota, Tennessee, Texas, Washington, and Wyoming.
- Some states have special reciprocal agreements with neighboring states. These agreements typically allow an employer operating in one state to withhold employees' personal income tax for the state in which they reside.
- Last, an employer may need to be concerned with other withholding tax requirements. Some states have counties with county tax requirements or cities with local income tax requirements.

Once an employer has determined its obligations to withhold

state taxes, it needs only to provide the new employee with his or her home state's version of the federal W-4 form. State income tax forms may be obtained from respective state revenue offices.[3] States without a state income tax will have no need for such a form.

Q: What is the requirement to report wages of employees who are collecting Social Security benefits?

Many older employees are choosing to continue to work past retirement age, and employers may wonder what their obligation may be to report wages when an employee says that he or she is collecting Social Security retirement benefits. To further complicate the issue, employees sometimes request that an employer either pays them less than the job calls for or keeps their hours to a minimum so their retirement benefits are not reduced.

An employer's obligation in this situation is to make sure that the employee is paid fairly and consistently with what others are paid for the same job. Requests to pay a lesser wage should be declined in light of the Equal Pay Act[4] and more recently the Lilly Ledbetter Fair Pay Act.[5]

Employment payroll taxes should continue to be taken out of the employee's paycheck, including Social Security and Medicare taxes. There is no obligation for an employer to report employee earnings to the Social Security Administration (SSA), as this is the responsibility of the employee.

To learn more about the earnings limits imposed by the SSA on retirement-eligible employees, see SSA Publication No. 05-10003.[6]

Finally, whether to accommodate an employee's request for fewer hours is a judgment call for the employer to make factoring in the needs of the business.

Q: Are bonuses taxable?

Bonuses are considered supplemental wages and therefore are taxable. As defined by the IRS in the *Employer's Tax Guide*, "Supplemental wages are compensation paid in addition to an employee's regular wages. They include, but are not limited to: bonuses, commissions, overtime pay, payments for accumulated sick leave, severance pay, awards, prizes, back pay, retroactive pay increases, and payments for nondeductible moving expenses."[7]

The amount of federal taxes withheld from the bonus depends on whether the bonus was combined with regular wages or was identified separately from the employee's wages. If an employer combines the bonus with the regular wages (and it is not identified separately), then the total amount (regular wages plus the bonus amount) will be taxed under one tax bracket.

Conversely, if the employer decides to separate the bonus from regular pay, the employer has two choices on taxing the bonus amount. The first option is to withhold a flat 25 percent tax from the bonus amount. The second option is to add the amount of the bonus to the last pay period's regular wages. Then, the employer will determine the amount of federal tax that would have been withheld from that total. Once the employer has the amount of taxes that would have been withheld if the bonus and regular wages were combined, the employer subtracts the amount of federal taxes already withheld from the regular pay. The difference in the tax amounts will be the amount withheld from the bonus check. For specific examples of the second option, see IRS Publication 15.[8]

Q: What tax issues should companies be aware of when giving employees a gift card or other small gift?

In the past employers could give employees cash or a cash equivalent gift such as a gift certificate for amounts less than $25 without any tax concern. These were known as de minimis fringe benefits or gifts.

That is no longer the case. The IRS tells employers that all fringe benefits, such as gift cards, are considered taxable wages unless specifically excluded by a section of the Internal Revenue Code.

Employers may still provide quite a few perks to employees that may be considered de minimis and not taxable to the employee. These include group meals, tickets to the theater or sporting events, traditional birthday gifts or holiday gifts with a low fair market value (not cash or cash equivalent), flowers, and occasional break treats such as coffee, doughnuts, soft drinks, and the like.

For example, the employer is able to give employees a small gift on the employee's birthday or give the employee a holiday turkey or ham without any taxable issues to the employee. However, if the employer gives the employee a gift certificate to purchase the item, it could create a situation in which the employee could receive cash back from the certificate and the gift would therefore no longer be considered a de minimis gift.

The IRS has created the *FSLG Fringe Benefit Guide* that addresses these fringe benefits, but also all other taxable fringe benefits employers might provide.[9] The guide along with the *Employer's Tax Guide to Fringe Benefits*, Publication 15-B,[10] are the IRS resources employers should reference when questioning any tax issues on employee fringe benefits.

Endnotes

Chapter 1

1. Internal Revenue Service, Form W-2, Wage and Tax Statement, http://www.irs.gov/pub/irs-pdf/fw2.pdf.

Chapter 2

1. Society for Human Resource Management, "Payment upon Termination," March 2013, http://www.shrm.org/LegalIssues/StateandLocalResources/StateandLocalStatutesandRegulations/Documents/paymentupontermination.pdf.
2. U.S. Department of Labor, "FairPay Regulations," http://www.dol.gov/whd/regs/compliance/fairpay/regulations.htm.
3. U.S. Department of Labor, "Wages and Hours Worked: Commissions," http://www.dol.gov/compliance/topics/wages-commissions.htm.

Chapter 3

1. New York State Department of Labor, "Notice of Pay Rate," http://www.labor.ny.gov/workerprotection/laborstandards/employer/wage-theft-prevention-act.shtm.
2. State of California, Department of Industrial Relations, "Wage Theft Protection Act," April 2013, https://www.dir.ca.gov/dlse/Governor_signs_Wage_Theft_Protection_Act_of_2011.html.
3. Allen Smith, "Final FLSA Rule Provides Guidance on Tip Credit Notice," Society for Human Resource Management,

April 8, 2011, http://www.shrm.org/LegalIssues/FederalRe-sources/Pages/FinalFLSARuleTipCreditNotice.aspx.

Chapter 4

1. Social Security Administration, "U.S. International Social Security Agreements," http://www.ssa.gov/international/agreements_overview.html.

2. Cornell University Law School, Legal Information Institute, "26 USC § 901: Taxes of Foreign Countries and of Possessions of United States," http://www.law.cornell.edu/uscode/text/26/901.

3. Internal Revenue Service, "Foreign Earned Income Exception," July 22, 2013, http://www.irs.gov/Individuals/International-Taxpayers/Foreign-Earned-Income-Exclusion.

4. Internal Revenue Service, Form 673: Statement for Claiming Exemption from Withholding on Foreign Earned Income Eligible for the Exclusion(s) Provided by Section 911, http://www.irs.gov/pub/irs-pdf/f673.pdf.

5. Internal Revenue Service, Form 2555: Foreign Earned Income, http://www.irs.gov/pub/irs-pdf/f2555.pdf.

6. Internal Revenue Service, Form 2555EZ: Foreign Earned Income Exclusion, http://www.irs.gov/pub/irs-pdf/f2555ez.pdf.

7. Social Security Administration, "U.S. International Social Security Agreements," http://www.ssa.gov/international/agreements_overview.html.

Chapter 5

1. Society for Human Resource Management, "Conducting Human Resource Audits," April 8, 2013, http://www.shrm.org/templatestools/toolkits/pages/humanresourceaudits.aspx.

2. United States Courts, "Chapter 11: Reorganization under the

Bankruptcy Code," http://www.uscourts.gov/FederalCourts/
Bankruptcy/BankruptcyBasics/Chapter11.aspx.

3. United States Courts, "Chapter 7: Liquidation under the Bank-
    ruptcy Code," http://www.uscourts.gov/FederalCourts/Bank-
    ruptcy/BankruptcyBasics/Chapter7.aspx.

4. Cornell University Law School, Legal Information Institute,
    "29 C.F.R. § 825.215: Equivalent Position," http://www.law.
    cornell.edu/cfr/text/29/825.215.

5. Ibid.

6. Internal Revenue Service, "Standard Mileage Rates for 2013,"
    http://www.irs.gov/uac/2013-Standard-Mileage-Rates-Up-
    1-Cent-per-Mile-for-Business,-Medical-and-Moving.

7. For example, see State of California, Department of Industrial
    Relations, "Travel Expense Reimbursements," http://www.dir.
    ca.gov/dlse/2802Regs/2802Regs-ProposedText13700-13706.
    pdf.

8. Society for Human Resource Management, "Collective Bar-
    gaining Agreement: What Is a Collective Bargaining Agree-
    ment?," June 1, 2012, http://www.shrm.org/templatestools/
    hrqa/pages/collectivebargainingagreement.aspx.

9. U.S. Department of Labor, "Fact Sheet #73: Break Time for
    Nursing Mothers under the FLSA," http://www.dol.gov/whd/
    regs/compliance/whdfs73.htm.

10. Gary C. Pierson and Sam R. Fulkerson, "March-April 1999:
    Older Workers Benefit Protection Act," Society for Human
    Resource Management, last reviewed December 2006, http://
    www.shrm.org/legalissues/legalreport/pages/cms_000947.aspx.

11. Society for Human Resource Management, "Age Discrimina-
    tion in Employment Act of 1967," http://www.shrm.org/legal-
    issues/federalresources/federalstatutesregulationsandguidanc/
    pages/agediscriminationinemploymentactof1967.aspx.

Chapter 6

1.   U.S. Department of Labor, "Fact Sheet #17G: Salary Basis Requirement and the Part 541 Exemptions under the Fair Labor Standards Act (FLSA)," last modified July 2008, http://www.dol.gov/whd/regs/compliance/fairpay/fs17g_salary.htm.

2.   Ibid.

3.   U.S. Department of Labor, "FLSA Overtime Calculator Advisor: Glossary: Compensatory Time Off," http://www.dol.gov/elaws/esa/flsa/otcalc/glossaryall.asp#Compensatory Time Off.

4.   Ibid.

5.   U.S. Department of Labor, "Fact Sheet #7: State and Local Governments under the Fair Labor Standards Act (FLSA)," http://www.dol.gov/whd/regs/compliance/whdfs7.pdf.

6.   Society for Human Resource Management, "Jury/Witness Duty Leave," last modified April 2013, http://www.shrm.org/LegalIssues/StateandLocalResources/StateandLocalStatutesandRegulations/Documents/statejurydutylaws.pdf.

7.   U.S. Department of Labor, "Fact Sheet #17A: Exemption for Executive, Administrative, Professional, Computer & Outside Sales Employees under the Fair Labor Standards Act (FLSA)," http://www.dol.gov/whd/regs/compliance/fairpay/fs17a_overview.pdf.

8.   U.S. Department of Labor, "Opinion Letters—Fair Labor Standards Act: FLSA2008-1NA," February 14, 2008, http://www.dol.gov/whd/opinion/FLSANA/2008/2008_02_14_01NA_FLSA.htm.

9.   U.S. Department of Labor, "Opinion Letters—Fair Labor Standards Act: FLSA2009-14," January 15, 2009, http://www.dol.gov/WHD/opinion/FLSA/2009/2009_01_15_14_FLSA.htm.

10. U.S. Department of Labor, "Fact Sheet #17G: Salary Basis Requirement and the Part 541 Exemptions under the Fair

Labor Standards Act (FLSA)," http://www.dol.gov/whd/regs/compliance/fairpay/fs17g_salary.pdf.

11. Cornell University Law School, Legal Information Institute, "29 C.F.R. § 541.101: Business Owner," http://www.law.cornell.edu/cfr/text/29/541.101.

12. Cornell University Law School, Legal Information Institute, "29 C.F.R. § 541.303: Teachers," http://www.law.cornell.edu/cfr/text/29/541.303.

13. Cornell University Law School, Legal Information Institute, "29 C.F.R. § 541.304: Practice of Law or Medicine," http://www.law.cornell.edu/cfr/text/29/541.304.

14. Cornell University Law School, Legal Information Institute, "29 C.F.R. § 541.500: General Rules for Outside Sales Employees," http://www.law.cornell.edu/cfr/text/29/541.500.

15. Cornell University Law School, Legal Information Institute, "29 C.F.R. § 541.709: Motion Picture Producing Industry," http://www.law.cornell.edu/cfr/text/29/541.709.

16. U.S. Department of Labor, FLSA 2006-6, March 10, 2006, http://www.dol.gov/whd/opinion/FLSA/2006/2006_03_10_06_FLSA.htm.

17. U.S. Department of Labor, "FLSA Hours Worked Advisor: Physical Exams, Fingerprinting and Drug Testing," http://www.dol.gov/elaws/esa/flsa/hoursworked/screenER13.asp.

18. U.S. Government Printing Office, "Title 29 C.F.R. § 541.118: Salary Basis," http://www.gpo.gov/fdsys/pkg/CFR-2000-title29-vol3/pdf/CFR-2000-title29-vol3-sec541-118-id537.pdf.

19. Cornell University Law School, Legal Information Institute, "29 C.F.R. § 785.19: Meal," http://www.law.cornell.edu/cfr/text/29/785.19.

20. Ibid.

21. Society for Human Resource Management, "Meal & Break:

Meal and Break Policy," last modified February 2010, http://www.shrm.org/TemplatesTools/Samples/Policies/Pages/CMS_009213.aspx.

22. U.S. Department of Labor, "Work Hours: Breaks & Meal Periods," http://www.dol.gov/dol/topic/workhours/breaks.htm.

23. Society for Human Resource Management, "State Meal/Rest Period Requirements," last modified July 2013, http://www.shrm.org/LegalIssues/StateandLocalResources/StateandLocal-StatutesandRegulations/Documents/statebreaklaws.pdf.

24. U.S. Department of Labor, "FLSA Hours Worked Advisor: Meal Periods and Rest Breaks," http://www.dol.gov/elaws/esa/flsa/hoursworked/screenEE4.asp.

25. U.S. Department of Labor, "FLSA Hours Worked Advisor: On-Call Time," http://www.dol.gov/elaws/esa/flsa/hoursworked/screenER80.asp.

26. U.S. Department of Labor, "Title 29 C.F.R. § 785: Hours Worked," reprinted May 2011, http://www.dol.gov/whd/regs/compliance/WH1312.pdf.

27. Society for Human Resource Management, "State and Local Statutes and Regulations," http://www.shrm.org/LegalIssues/StateandLocalResources/StateandLocalStatutesandRegulations/Pages/default.aspx.

28. U.S. Department of Labor, "Fact Sheet #22: Hours Worked under the Fair Labor Standards Act (FLSA)," last modified July 2008, http://www.dol.gov/whd/regs/compliance/whdfs22.pdf.

29. U.S. Department of Labor, "Fact Sheet #17G: Salary Basis Requirement and the Part 541 Exemptions under the Fair Labor Standards Act (FLSA)," last modified July 2008, http://www.dol.gov/whd/regs/compliance/fairpay/fs17g_salary.pdf.

30. U.S. Department of Labor, "ESA Final Rule: Defining and

Delimiting the Exemptions for Executive, Administrative, Professional, Outside Sales and Computer Employees; Final Rule," April 23, 2004, http://www.dol.gov/whd/regs/compliance/fairpay/regulations_final.htm.

31. U.S. Department of Labor, "Fact Sheet #22: Hours Worked under the Fair Labor Standards Act (FLSA)," last modified July 2008, http://www.dol.gov/whd/regs/compliance/whdfs22.pdf.

32. Cornell University Law School, Legal Information Institute, "29 C.F.R. § 785.17: On-Call Time," http://www.law.cornell.edu/cfr/text/29/785.17.

33. Ibid.

34. Ibid.

35. Cornell University Law School, Legal Information Institute, "29 C.F.R. § 541.604: Minimum Guarantee Plus Extras," http://www.law.cornell.edu/cfr/text/29/541.604.

36. U.S. Department of Labor, "Fact Sheet #22."

37. U.S. Department of Labor, "Fact Sheet #22: Hours Worked Under the Fair Labor Standards Act (FLSA)," http://www.dol.gov/whd/regs/compliance/whdfs22.pdf.

38. Cornell University Law School, Legal Information Institute, "29 C.F.R. § 785.35: Home to Work; Ordinary Situation," http://www.law.cornell.edu/cfr/text/29/785.35.

39. Cornell University Law School, Legal Information Institute, "29 C.F.R. § 785.39: Travel away from Home Community," http://www.law.cornell.edu/cfr/text/29/785.39.

40. Society for Human Resource Management, "Hours of Work," http://www.shrm.org/LegalIssues/StateandLocalResources/StateandLocalStatutesandRegulations/Documents/Hoursofwork.pdf.

41. Cornell University Law School, Legal Information Institute,

"29 C.F.R. § 785.41: Work Performed while Traveling," http://www.law.cornell.edu/cfr/text/29/785.41.

42. U.S. Department of Labor, "Wage and Hour Advisory Memorandum No. 2006-2," May 31, 2006, http://www.dol.gov/whd/FieldBulletins/AdvisoryMemo2006_2.htm.

43. Ibid.

44. Ibid.

45. *IBP v. Alvarez*, 546 U.S. 21 (2005).

46. Sandra Sipari, "Effects of Portal-To-Portal Act on Determination of Hours Worked under the FLSA," Society for Human Resource Management, July 1, 2002, http://www.shrm.org/hrdisciplines/compensation/articles/pages/cms_000089.aspx.

47. U.S. Department of Labor, "Fact Sheet #22."

48. U.S. Department of Labor, *Handy Reference Guide to the Fair Labor Standards Act*, http://www.dol.gov/whd/regs/compliance/wh1282.pdf.

49. U.S. Department of Labor, "Fact Sheet #22."

50. U.S. Department of Labor, "Minimum Wage Laws in the States - January 1, 2013," http://www.dol.gov/whd/minwage/america.htm.

51. Society for Human Resource Management, "Overtime: Calculation: We Would Like to Have a Nonexempt Employee Work Two Jobs with a Different Hourly Rate of Pay. Which Rate of Pay Is Used to Calculate the Employee's Overtime Pay?," December 11, 2012, http://www.shrm.org/TemplatesTools/hrqa/Pages/WewouldliketohaveanonexemptemployeeworktwojobswithadifferenthourlyrateofpayWhichrateofpayisusedtocalculatetheemployee'sover.aspx.

52. *Walling v. Portland Terminal Co.*, 330 U.S. 148 (1947).

53. U.S. Department of Labor, "Rulings and Interpretations," http://www.dol.gov/whd/opinion/opinion.htm.

54. U.S. Internal Revenue Service, "Topic 762 - Independent Contractor vs. Employee," last modified August 29, 2013, http://www.irs.gov/taxtopics/tc762.html.

55. U.S. Department of Labor, "Fair Labor Standards Act Advisor: Independent Contractors," http://www.dol.gov/elaws/esa/flsa/docs/contractors.asp.

56. U.S. Department of Labor, "Fair Labor Standards Act Advisor: Volunteers," http://www.dol.gov/elaws/esa/flsa/docs/volunteers.asp.

57. U.S. Department of Labor, "Fair Labor Standards Act Advisor: Am I Covered by the FLSA?," http://www.dol.gov/elaws/esa/flsa/scope/screen10.asp.

58. Cornell University, Law Information Institute, "29 C.F.R. § 531.29: Board, Lodging, or Other Facilities," http://www.law.cornell.edu/cfr/text/29/531.29.

59. Cornell University, Law Information Institute, "29 C.F.R. § 531.27: Payment in Cash or Its Equivalent Required," http://www.law.cornell.edu/cfr/text/29/531.27.

60. Cornell University, Law Information Institute, "29 C.F.R. § 531.32: Other Facilities," http://www.law.cornell.edu/cfr/text/29/531.32.

61. Cornell University, Law Information Institute, "29 C.F.R. § 541.700: Primary Duty," http://www.law.cornell.edu/cfr/text/29/541.700.

62. Cornell University, Law Information Institute, "29 C.F.R. § 516.23: Employees of Hospitals and Residential Care Facilities Compensated for Overtime Work on the Basis of a 14-Day Work Period Pursuant to Section 7(j) of the Act," http://www.law.cornell.edu/cfr/text/29/516.23.

63. Cornell University, Law Information Institute, "29 C.F.R. § 778.104: Each Workweek Stands Alone," http://www.law.

cornell.edu/cfr/text/29/778.104.

64. Cornell University, Law Information Institute, "29 C.F.R. § 785.11: General," http://www.law.cornell.edu/cfr/text/29/785.11.

65. Cornell University, Law Information Institute, "29 C.F.R. § 785.13: Duty of Management," http://www.law.cornell.edu/cfr/text/29/785.13.

66. Cornell University, Law Information Institute, "29 C.F.R. § 541.602: Salary Basis," http://www.law.cornell.edu/cfr/text/29/541.602.

67. Cornell University, Law Information Institute, "29 C.F.R. § 541.700: Primary Duty," http://www.law.cornell.edu/cfr/text/29/541.700.

68. Society for Human Resource Management, "Overtime Laws," last modified June 2013, http://www.shrm.org/Legal-Issues/StateandLocalResources/StateandLocalStatutesand-Regulations/Documents/OvertimeLaws.pdf.

69. Society for Human Resource Management, "Bonus: What Is the Difference between a Discretionary and a Nondiscretionary Bonus?," December 11, 2012, http://www.shrm.org/Tem-platesTools/hrqa/pages/iscretionaryvsnondiscretionarybonus.aspx.

70. Ibid.

71. Cornell University, Law Information Institute, "29 C.F.R. § 778.208-215: Inclusion and Exclusion of Bonuses in Computing the 'Regular Rate,' " http://www.law.cornell.edu/cfr/text/29/778.208.

72. Cornell University, Law Information Institute, "29 C.F.R. § 778.209: Method of Inclusion of Bonus in Regular Rate," http://www.law.cornell.edu/cfr/text/29/778.209.

73. Cornell University, Law Information Institute, "29 C.F.R.

§ 779.18: Regular Rate," http://www.law.cornell.edu/cfr/text/29/779.18.

74. U.S. Department of Labor, "Wages: Overtime Pay," http://www.dol.gov/dol/topic/wages/overtimepay.htm.

75. U.S. Department of Labor, "FLSA Hours Worked Advisor: Suffer or Permit to Work," http://www.dol.gov/elaws/esa/flsa/hoursworked/screen1d.asp.

76. Cornell University, Law Information Institute, "29 CFR 825.104 - Covered employer," http://www.law.cornell.edu/cfr/text/29/825.104.

77. U.S. Department of Labor, "Fair Labor Standards Act Advisor: Volunteers," http://www.dol.gov/elaws/esa/flsa/docs/volunteers.asp.

78. U.S. Department of Labor, "Fact Sheet #7: State and Local Governments Under the Fair Labor Standards Act (FLSA)," http://www.dol.gov/whd/regs/compliance/whdfs7.pdf.

79. U.S. Department of Labor, "Fair Labor Standards Act Advisor: Public Sector Volunteers," http://www.dol.gov/elaws/esa/flsa/docs/publicvol.asp.

80. Cornell University, Law Information Institute, "29 C.F.R. § 541.602: Salary Basis," http://www.law.cornell.edu/cfr/text/29/541.602.

81. U.S. Department of Labor, "FLSA Overtime Security Advisor: Compensation Requirements," http://www.dol.gov/elaws/esa/flsa/overtime/cr4.htm.

82. Cornell University, Law Information Institute, "29 C.F.R. § 541.602: Salary Basis," http://www.law.cornell.edu/cfr/text/29/541.602.

83. U.S. Government Printing Office, "Title 29 C.F.R. § 541.118," http://www.gpo.gov/fdsys/pkg/CFR-2000-title29-vol3/pdf/CFR-2000-title29-vol3-sec541-118-id537.pdf.

84. Society for Human Resource Management, "Federal Statutes, Regulations, and Guidance," http://www.shrm.org/LegalIssues/FederalResources/FederalStatutesRegulationsandGuidanc/Pages/default.aspx.
85. Society for Human Resource Management, "State and Local Statutes and Regulations," http://www.shrm.org/legalissues/stateandlocalresources/stateandlocalstatutesandregulations/pages/default.aspx.
86. Society for Human Resource Management, "State Call-In/Call-Back/Reporting Pay Laws," http://www.shrm.org/LegalIssues/StateandLocalResources/StateandLocalStatutesandRegulations/Documents/Callbackcallinreportingpay.pdf.
87. U.S. Department of Labor, "Fact Sheet #22: Hours Worked under the Fair Labor Standards Act (FLSA)," http://www.dol.gov/whd/regs/compliance/whdfs22.htm.
88. Cornell University, Law Information Institute, "29 C.F.R. § 541.603," Effect of Improper Deductions from Salary, http://www.law.cornell.edu/cfr/text/29/541.603.
89. Ibid.
90. Society for Human Resource Management, "Vacation/Sick/PTO Laws," last modified June 2013, http://www.shrm.org/LegalIssues/StateandLocalResources/StateandLocalStatutesandRegulations/Documents/VacationPTOLaws.pdf.
91. U.S. Department of Labor, "Opinion Letters: Fair Labor Standards Act: FLSA2009-2," January 14, 2009, http://www.dol.gov/whd/opinion/FLSA/2009/2009_01_14_02_FLSA.pdf.
92. U.S. Department of Labor, "Opinion Letters: Fair Labor Standards Act: FLSA2005-41," October 24, 2005, http://www.wageandhourcounsel.com/uploads/file/FLSA2005-41.pdf.
93. Cornell University, Law Information Institute, "29 C.F.R. § 541.602: Salary Basis," http://www.law.cornell.edu/cfr/

text/29/541.602.

94. *Auer v. Robbins*, 519 U.S. 452 (1997)

95. Cornell University, Law Information Institute, "29 C.F.R. § 541.602: Salary Basis," http://www.law.cornell.edu/cfr/text/29/541.602.

96. U.S. Department of Labor, "Youth & Labor: Exemptions to FLSA," http://www.dol.gov/dol/topic/youthlabor/exemptions-FLSA.htm.

97. U.S. Department of Labor, "State Labor Laws," http://www.dol.gov/whd/state/state.htm.

98. 98. U.S. Department of Labor, "Youth & Labor: Hazardous Jobs," http://www.dol.gov/dol/topic/youthlabor/hazardous-jobs.htm.

99. U.S. Department of Labor, "Youth & Labor: Agricultural Employment," http://www.dol.gov/dol/topic/youthlabor/Agriculturalemployment.htm.

100. U.S. Department of Labor, "Fact Sheet #34: Hazardous Occupations Order No. 2. Youth Employment Provision and Driving Automobiles and Trucks under the Fair Labor Standards (FLSA)," last modified July 2008, http://www.dol.gov/whd/regs/compliance/whdfs34.htm.

101. U.S. Department of Labor, "Youth & Labor: Employment by Parents," http://www.dol.gov/dol/topic/youthlabor/employmentparents.htm.

102. U.S. Department of Labor, "Fair Labor Standards Act Advisor: Work Experience and Career Exploration Program," http://www.dol.gov/elaws/esa/flsa/docs/wecep.asp.

103. U.S. Department of Labor, "Fair Labor Standards Act Advisor: Youth Minimum Wage Program," http://www.dol.gov/elaws/esa/flsa/docs/ymwplink.asp.

104. U.S. Department of Labor, "Youth & Labor: Hazardous Jobs,"

http://www.dol.gov/dol/topic/youthlabor/hazardousjobs.htm.

105. U.S. Department of Labor, "Youth & Labor: Work Permits & Age Certificates," http://www.dol.gov/dol/topic/youthlabor/workpermitsagecert.htm.

106. U.S. Department of Labor, "FLSA—Child Labor Rules Advisor: Welcome to the Fair Labor Standards Act (FLSA) Child Labor Rules Advisor," http://www.dol.gov/elaws/esa/flsa/cl/default.htm.

107. U.S. Department of Labor, "Child Labor Requirements In Agricultural Occupations Under the Fair Labor Standards Act (Child Labor Bulletin 102)," last modified June 2007, http://www.dol.gov/whd/regs/compliance/childlabor102.pdf.

108. U.S. Department of Labor, "Youth & Labor: Age Requirements," http://www.dol.gov/dol/topic/youthlabor/agerequirements.htm.

Chapter 7

1. U.S. Department of Labor, "VETS USERRA Fact Sheet 3," http://www.dol.gov/vets/programs/userra/userra_fs.htm.

2. Cornell University, Law Information Institute, "29 C.F.R. § 541.602: Salary Basis," http://www.law.cornell.edu/cfr/text/29/541.602.

3. Ibid.

4. John F. Buckley and Ronald M. Green, *State by State Guide to Human Resources Law* (New York: Aspen Publishers, annual edition).

Chapter 8

1. Society for Human Resource Management, "Payment of Wages/Direct Deposit Law," last modified July 2013, http://www.shrm.org/LegalIssues/StateandLocalResources/Statean-

dLocalStatutesandRegulations/Documents/wagepaymentlaw. pdf.

2.   Internal Revenue Service, "Federal Income Tax Withholding," last modified-April 22, 2013, http://www.irs.gov/Individuals/ International-Taxpayers/Federal-Income-Tax-Withholding.

3.   Society for Human Resource Management, "Federal Insurance Contributions Act (FICA) of 1935," last modified October 7, 2008, http://www.shrm.org/legalissues/federalresources/ federalstatutesregulationsandguidanc/pages/federalinsurancec ontributionsact(fica)of1935.aspx.

4.   Internal Revenue Service, "Federal Unemployment Tax," last modified July 26, 2013, http://www.irs.gov/Individuals/ International-Taxpayers/Federal-Unemployment-Tax.

5.   Society for Human Resource Management, "Vacation/Sick/ PTO Laws," last modified June 2013, http://www.shrm.org/ LegalIssues/StateandLocalResources/StateandLocalStatute- sandRegulations/Documents/VacationPTOLaws.pdf.

6.   Society for Human Resource Management, "COBRA: Model Election Form and Notice," July 12, 2013, http://www. shrm.org/TemplatesTools/Samples/HRForms/Articles/Pages/ COBRAElectionandNotice.aspx; Society for Human Resource Management, "Consolidated Omnibus Budget Reconciliation Act (COBRA) of 1986," last modified July 12, 2013, http:// www.shrm.org/legalissues/federalresources/federalstatutesreg- ulationsandguidanc/pages/consolidatedomnibusbudgetreconcil iationact(cobra)of1986.aspx.

7.   U.S. Department of Labor, "Fact Sheet #23: Overtime Pay Requirements of the FLSA" last revised July 2008, http://www. dol.gov/whd/regs/compliance/whdfs23.htm.

8.   Ibid.

9.   U.S. Department of the Treasury, Financial Management Ser-

vice, "Overview: ACH," http://www.fms.treas.gov/ach/index.html.

10. Internal Revenue Service, "Hiring Employees," last modified September 3, 2013, http://www.irs.gov/Businesses/Small-Businesses-&-Self-Employed/Hiring-Employees.

11. U.S. Citizenship and Immigration Services "I-9, Employment Eligibility Verification," http://www.uscis.gov/portal/site/uscis/menuitem.5af9bb95919f35e66f614176543f6d1a/?vgnextoid=31b3ab0a43b5d010VgnVCM10000048f3d6a1RCRD&vgnextchannel=db029c7755cb9010VgnVCM10000045f3d6a1RCRD.

12. Social Security Administration, "Social Security Card and Number," http://www.ssa.gov/ssnumber/.

13. U.S. Department of Labor, "Fact Sheet #22: Hours Worked Under the Fair Labor Standards Act (FLSA)," last modified July 2008, http://www.dol.gov/whd/regs/compliance/whdfs22.pdf.

14. Internal Revenue Service, "Hiring Employees," last modified September 3, 2013, http://www.irs.gov/Businesses/Small-Businesses-&-Self-Employed/Hiring-Employees.

15. Society for Human Resource Management, "State and Local Statutes and Regulations," http://www.shrm.org/LegalIssues/StateandLocalResources/StateandLocalStatutesandRegulations/Pages/default.aspx.

16. U.S. Department of Labor, "Wages: Recordkeeping & Reporting," http://www.dol.gov/dol/topic/wages/wagesrecordkeeping.htm.

Chapter 9

1. Society for Human Resource Management, "How to Calculate Overtime Rates for Shift Differentials," December 10, 2010,

http://www.shrm.org/TemplatesTools/HowtoGuides/Pages/CalculateshiftdiffOT.aspx.

2. Cornell University, Law Information Institute, "29 C.F.R. § 785.36: Home to Work in Emergency Situations," http://www.law.cornell.edu/cfr/text/29/785.36.

3. Society for Human Resource Management, "Hours of Work," http://www.shrm.org/LegalIssues/StateandLocalResources/StateandLocalStatutesandRegulations/Documents/Hoursofwork.pdf.

4. Society for Human Resource Management, "Overtime Laws," last modified June 2013, http://www.shrm.org/LegalIssues/StateandLocalResources/StateandLocalStatutesandRegulations/Documents/OvertimeLaws.pdf.

5. Ibid.

6. U.S. Department of Labor, "Wages: Hazard Pay," http://www.dol.gov/dol/topic/wages/hazardpay.htm.

7. Act of July 2, 1890 (Sherman Anti-Trust Act), July 2, 1890; Enrolled Acts and Resolutions of Congress, 1789-1992; General Records of the United States Government; Record Group 11; National Archives, http://www.ourdocuments.gov/doc.php?flash=true&doc=51.

8. U.S. Department of Labor, Bureau of Labor Statistics, http://www.bls.gov/.

9. Society for Human Resource Management, "Express Requests: Salary Survey Directory," http://apps.shrm.org/hrresources/ExpressRequests.aspx?type=4.

10. Society for Human Resource Management, Compensation Data Center, http://www.shrm.org/Research/SHRMCompensationDataService/Pages/default.aspx.

Chapter 10

1. Internal Revenue Service, Form 1099-MISC, http://www.irs.gov/pub/irs-pdf/f1099msc.pdf.

2. Internal Revenue Service, Instructions for Form 1099-MISC, http://www.irs.gov/pub/irs-pdf/i1099msc.pdf.

3. Society for Human Resource Management, "State Income Tax Offices," http://www.shrm.org/LegalIssues/StateandLocalRe-sources/StateandLocalStatutesandRegulations/Pages/StateIn-comeTaxOffices.aspx.

4. Society for Human Resource Management, "Equal Pay Act of 1963," http://www.shrm.org/LegalIssues/FederalResources/FederalStatutesRegulationsandGuidanc/Pages/EqualPayAc-tof1963.aspx.

5. Society for Human Resource Management, "Lilly Ledbetter Fair Pay Act of 2007," http://www.shrm.org/LegalIssues/Fed-eralResources/FederalStatutesRegulationsandGuidanc/Pages/LillyLedbetterFairPayActof2007.aspx.

6. Social Security Administration, *Update 2013*, SSA Publication No. 05-10003, http://ssa.gov/pubs/EN-05-10003.pdf.

7. Internal Revenue Service, "(Circular E), Employer's Tax Guide," for use in 2013, http://www.irs.gov/pub/irs-pdf/p15.pdf.

8. Ibid.

9. Internal Revenue Service, "FSLG: Fringe Benefit Guide," http://www.irs.gov/pub/irs-tege/fringe_benefit_fslg_2013.pdf.

10. Internal Revenue Service, *Employer's Tax Guide to Fringe Benefits*, 2003, Publication No. 15-B, http://www.irs.gov/pub-lications/p15b/index.html.

Index

A

abandonment period, 108, 109

absence(s), 37, 46, 54, 59, 88, 90, 93, 100

    military-related, 99

    partial-day, 86, 87, 93

    partial-week, 99

ad hoc approach, 28

adjustments, 131

advance, 11

age certificates, 98

Age Discrimination in Employment Act, 41

age requirements, 96

Americans with Disabilities Act (ADA), 46

antitrust violations, 125

attendance, 45, 95

audit(s), 33, 109

auditor(s), 33, 34, 50, 109

Automated Clearing House, 105

awards, 8, 135

B

balance sheet approach, 25, 26

balance sheet method, 26

bankruptcy, 35, 36

beneficiary designations, 104

benefit days, 54

benefits, fringe, 136

    de minimis, 136

    taxable, 136

benefits, paid time-off, 99, 100

benefits, Social Security retirement, 134

bilateral Social Security agreement, *see* totalization agreement

billable hours, 52

binational agreement, *see* totalization agreement

board, 72, 73

bona fide meal periods, 55, 57

bona fide residence test, 30

bonus(es), 22, 23, 37, 79, 119, 135; *see also* chapter 1

    anniversary, 79

attendance, 79
discretionary, 7, 78, 79
eligibility, 9
gift, 79
holiday, 79
nondiscretionary, 7, 78, 79
plan, 8
production-oriented, 79
retention, 79
spontaneous ("spot"
   awards), 79
break(s), 40, 56
breast-feeding, 39, 40
broadband pay structure, 122
buildup system, *see* balance
   sheet approach
Bureau of Labor Statistics (BLS),
   126
business
   closures, 93, 94
   goals, 116, 128
   strategy, 115

C
cafeteria plans approach, 25, 27
capital gain, 127
capital loss, 127
carryover, 110
cash flow, 14
Chapter 11, 35
Chapter 7, 35, 36

COBRA, 41, 104
collective bargaining, 39, 73, 78,
   82, 111,128
commission(s), 22, 23, 35, 36,
   135; *see also* chapter 2
   flat rate, 16
   payments, 13
   plan agreement, 13
   variable rate, 16
compa-ratio, 123, 124
compensation
   direct, 21
   disguised, 8
   indirect, 21
   perspective, 26
   philosophy, 19, 20, 116,
      117
   policies, 34
   program, 121
   review period, 19
   strategy/ies, 113, 114, 115
   structure, 113
   system, 120
compensatory time (comp time),
   46, 47
competency-based plan, 25
competitive outlook, 116
compressed workweek(s), 75,
   103
consumption patterns, 25
cost-of-living, 26, 36

credits, 131

D

dangerous behavior, 95

deceased employee, 103

deductible loss, 127

deduction(s), 59, 94, 99, 131

    benefit, 111

    improper, 91, 92

    itemized, 30

    partial-day wage, 86

    salary, 95

    wage, 93

differential pay practices, 117

direct deposit(s), 105

dirty duty, 117

disciplinary action, 94

disciplinary suspensions, 94

discipline, 62, 112

discrimination, 75, 112

discriminatory claims, 94

dissatisfaction, 114

doffing, 65, 66, 67

donning, 65, 66, 67

draw, 11, 12, 13, 14

drug testing, 52

E

employment agreement, 13

employment contract, 78

engaged to wait, 60

Equal Pay Act, 134

exempt status, 23, 33, 43, 45, 46, 47, 48, 49, 51, 52, 53, 54, 58, 59, 61, 62, 74, 86, 87, 88, 89, 90, 91, 93, 94, 99

exemptions, 50, 63, 96, 131

expatriate(s), 25, 26, 27, 28

F

Fair Labor Standards Act (FLSA), 14, 15, 22-3, 34, 36, 40, 41, 99, 105, 107, 111, 112, 117, 118, 131; *see also* chapter 6

Family and Medical Leave Act (FMLA), 36, 59, 86, 87, 89

Federal Income Tax Withholding (FITW), 104

Federal Insurance Contributions Act (FICA), 104

Federal Unemployment Tax Act (FUTA), 104

flexible scheduling, 46, 52

foreign assignment, 26

forfeiture, 110

Form 1099-MISC, 132

Form 2555, 30

Form 2555EZ, 30

Form 673, 30

Form W-2, 8, 106

Form W-4, 131, 132, 134

G

gift certificate, 135

guarantee, *see* nonrecoverable
   draw

H

hazardous
   duty, 117
   jobs, 97
   occupations, 96
hourly basis, 48, 53, 58
human capital needs, 116

I

I-9, 107, 108
IBP v. Alvarez, 66
incentive(s), 25
   earnings, 14
   payments, 14
   relocation, 26
   stock options (ISO), 126,
      127
inclement weather, 89, 90, 91
income, 8, 30, 126, 127
independent contractors, 72
information sharing, 125
interim assignments, 119, 120
interim role(s), 119, 120
intern(s), 70, 71, 72

Internal Revenue Service (IRS),
   29, 30, 38, 72, 106, 107, 108,
   127, 132, 133, 135, 136
internship, 71

J

job(s)
   descriptions, 34
   duties, 87, 95
   evaluation(s), 25, 120, 121
   part-time, 48
   reinstatement rights, 99
   worth, 20
jury duty, 47, 88

L

labor costs, 113, 114
labor markets, 113, 114, 115
lactation breaks, 38-9, 40
laissez faire approach, 27
leadership team, 117
leave(s), 37
   accrued, 93
   bank, 46, 91, 100
   days, 54
   eligibility, 110
   family, 36, 38
   FMLA, 37
   holiday, 67
   intermittent, 59, 89
   medical, 36, 38

military, 99, 100

non-FMLA, 37

paid, 11, 12, 90

personal, 103

plan, 86

policy, 55

sick, 67, 86, 135

status, 37

time, 54

vacation, 37, 67, 109-110

Lilly Ledbetter Fair Pay Act, 134

liquidation, 35

localization approach, 25, 26, 27

lodging, 72, 73

lump sum approach, 25

M

market conditions, 116

market surveys, 25

meals, 55, 56, 56, 58, 84

meaningful presentation, 8

merit, 25

   budget, 123

   increase, 122

   program, 121

mileage reimbursements, 38

military, 88, 99

misconduct, 45

morale, 9, 46, 114

N

natural disasters, 54

negotiation approach, 25, 26

new-hire orientation, 62

nondeductible moving expenses, 135

nonexempt status, 23, 33, 43, 44, 45, 50, 53, 58, 59, 61, 63, 64, 67, 69, 70, 74, 75, 78, 80, 82, 89, 91, 94, 105

O

off-duty status, 60

off-the-clock work, 84

Older Workers Benefit Protection Act, 41

on the clock, 66

on-call, 56, 57, 59-60, 61, 68

operating objectives, 116

organizational philosophy, 19, 122

organizational policy, 20

outplacement services, 41

outside sales employees, 15

overtime, 23, 44, 45, 49, 50, 53, 54, 61, 67, 72, 74, 75, 76, 77, 78, 80, 81, 82, 83, 87, 95, 96, 105, 118

   calculations, 76, 78, 79

   compensation, 72

   compliance, 33

mandatory, 82
pay, 48, 50, 70, 80, 79, 91,
   92, 135
payment, 83
requirements, 14
straight time (STOT), 62
unauthorized, 77

P

paid leave benefits, *see* chapter 7
paid time off (PTO), 80, 90, 93,
   94, 99, 104
part-time status, 48
Patient Protection and
   Affordable Care Act, 38
pay day traditions, 106
pay
   base, 13
   call-in, 53
   differential, 117, 119
   hazard, 119
   holiday, 103
   premium, 117, 119
   rates, 114
   report-in pay, 53, 89, 90
   retroactive, 135
   severance, 135
   strategy, 115
   supplemental, 120
   variable, 22
paychecks, 108, 109

payroll, 34, 105; *see also*
   chapter 8
performance, 7, 9, 14, 20, 27,
   45, 52, 62, 63, 122, 124
   appraisals, 120
   evaluations, 78, 120
   issues, 95
   measures, 16
   poor, 114
   rating, 123
physical presence test, 30
Portal-to-Portal Act, 66
premiums, 118
prevailing marketplace, 114
primary duty, 51, 74
prizes, 135
productivity, 7, 46, 114
profit-sharing plans, 79
protected class, 7

R

ramp-up, 14
reorganization, 35
repatriation, 26
rest, 55, 56
retaliation, 37, 99
retention tool, 126

S

safe harbor policy, 92
safe harbor rules, 91, 92

safety infraction, 94
safety rule(s), 87, 88
salaried, 43, 45
    exempt, 88, 99
    nonexempt, 44, 77, 78
salary/ies, 35, 36, 43
    base, 25
    basis, 45, 48, 49, 50,51,
        54, 61, 62, 74, 78, 87,
        88, 93, 95, 96, 99
    deductions, 54
    home-country, 25
    increase budget, 122
    range, 19, 20
    requirement, 51
sales plan, 15
severance, 40, 41
sexual harassment, 95
Sherman Anti-Trust Act of
    1890, 125
shift differential(s), 22, 23, 79,
    117, 118
sick day, 83
Social Security Administration,
    107, 134
Social Security card, 106, 107,
    108
Social Security Number (SSN),
    106
stock, 126, 127
    incentive plan, 126

    option, 127
succession planning process, 20

T

tangible personal property, 8
tax(es)
    alternative minimum, 127
    equalization program, 28
    expense, 28
    foreign, 28
    income, 29, 30, 133
    Medicare, 30, 134
    payroll, 107
    protection approach, 28
    Social Security, 28, 29, 30,
        134
    treatment, 126
    withholding, 133
tax-exempt reimbursements, 38
telecommuting, 46
terminal week, 95
terminated employees, 13
termination(s), 8, 9, 12, 13, 16,
    59, 100, 110, 111
time clock, 112
time records, 84
timekeeping, 66
    guidelines, 112
    method, 82
    policies, 84
    records, 84

systems, 84

timesheet, 112

tipped employees, 22

tips, 22, 23

total compensation, 15, 21

total reward(s) strategy/ies, 116,
 127, 128, 129

totalization agreement(s), 29, 30

trainee(s), 71

training, 62, 63, 64, 65, 67, 68,
 71, 129

travel, 38, 64, 65, 67, 68, 69,
 70, 73, 118

trusts, 79

turnover, 114

U

U.S. Bankruptcy Court, 35, 36

U.S. Department of Labor
 (DOL), 33, 34, 36, 44, 45,
 46, 47, 48, 51, 52, 53, 54, 56,
 60, 62, 69, 71, 72, 84, 85, 95,
 98, 107

unclaimed property, 108, 109

Uniformed Services
 Employment and
 Reemployment Rights Act
 (USERRA), 99, 100

union contract, 94

unionization efforts, 114

unique protective gear, 65, 66,
 67

unpaid disciplinary suspension,
 88

unpaid workers, 84

V

vacation
 accrued, 100, 110
 days, 54
 hours, 110
 pay, 100
 payout, 109, 110
 policy, 55
 time, 99, 100

vesting, 126

volunteer services, 84, 86

volunteers, 85

W

Wage and Hour Division, 69

wage and hour
 implications, 56
 laws, 46, 100
 lawsuit, 83
 violations, 33

wage(s), 35, 36
 communication, 22
 deduction laws, 111
 hourly, 44

minimum, 11, 14, 22, 33, 44, 49, 50, 53, 61, 69, 70, 72, 73, 74, 78, 84, 94, 95, 96

notices, 22

rate(s), 22, 94

requirements, 96

taxable, 136

total 11, 12

unclaimed, 109

waiting to be engaged, 60, 61

walking time, 66

Walling v. Portland Terminal Co., 71

weather-related closures, 89

withholding allowance, 132

withholding tax requirements, 133

Work Experience and Career Exploration Program (WECEP), 97

work

call back, 117

hours, 52, 96

permits, 98

shift, 117

unauthorized, 77

weekend, 117

workplace conduct rules, 45, 94, 95

workplace emergency, 118

Y

youth, 96

Additional
SHRM-Published Books

Becoming the Evidence-Based Manager:
Making the Science of Management Work for You
  Gary P. Latham

Business Literacy Survival Guide for HR Professionals
  Regan W. Garey

Business-Focused HR: 11 Processes to Drive Results
  Scott P. Mondore, Shane S. Douthitt, and Marissa A. Carson

The Essential Guide to Federal Employment Laws
  Lisa Guerin and Amy DelPo

Global Compensation and Benefits:
Developing Policies for Local Nationals
  Roger Herod

Hidden Drivers of Success:
Leveraging Employee Insights for Strategic Advantage
  William A. Schiemann, Jerry H. Seibert, and Brian S. Morgan

Human Resource Essentials:
Your Guide to Starting and Running the HR Function
  Lin Grensing-Pophal

The Manager's Guide to HR: Hiring, Firing, Performance Evaluations,
Documentation, Benefits, and Everything Else You Need to Know
  Max Muller

The Power of Stay Interviews for Engagement and Retention
  Richard P. Finnegan

SHRM Human Capital Benchmarking
  Society for Human Resource Management